FOREWORD

While reading this book you will be absorbed in the life and times of the first African American to lead a major sports organization: Mr. Robert W. Lee. Mr. Lee was one of the founders and the first president of the International Boxing Federation, an organization that challenged the status quo in the boxing industry. Mr. Lee loved boxing and all of the excitement that went along with it. He mingled with the president of South Africa Nelson Mandela and dined with the president of the Phillippines Ferdinand Marcos. He did all that he could to help his organization become recognized as a legitimate competitor in boxing.

As a Black man, Mr. Lee faced many challenges as he navigated through the racism launched at him during his tenure as the leader of the IBF. However, Robert W. Lee would not be deterred. He became a champion in his own right. I met Robert W. Lee over fifteen years ago in New Jersey when I encouraged him to share his story with the world. I explained to him how his story would be an inspiration not only to young African American men but also an encouragement to anyone who has a dream or goal that seems impossible to achieve. Mr. Lee shows us how a man from humble beginnings would eventually become one of the most powerful men in the United States and beyond in the world of boxing.

As Robert Lee's spiritual advisor and friend, I was blessed to be invited to write the foreword for The Final Round- Round 16. Bob and I connected because, like myself, he is a spiritual man who confesses his love for God and acknowledges from where his blessings flow. Bob says, "I thank God for blessings 200,594", according to him the number of blessings he's received thus far. After sharing with me how his career got started and our mutual love for boxing, I looked forward to the stories Mr. Lee shared about the sport that he loved.

Reminiscing, he would tell me stories of how he got Joe Louis' autograph on a napkin while working at the golf course as a young man. He talked about Jersey Joe Walcott, Ezzard Charles, Rocky Marciano, and of course the great Muhammad Ali. Hearing his stories made me feel like I was there when he interacted with some of the greats in boxing. There is no doubt that Robert W. Lee has earned his place in history and deserved to be inducted into the Boxing Hall of Fame.

Our love for boxing allowed us to develop a lifelong friendship and our love for God made him my brother in Christ. The Final Round- Round 16 will allow readers to experience the triumphs and the tragedies of one of America's greatest sports legend Robert W. Lee.

Gerald King,
CEO of Operation Care Outreach Nursing Home Ministry
Fort Wayne, Indiana

THE
FINAL ROUND

ROUND 16

ROBERT W. LEE MEMOIRS
LISA MAYDWELL

I would like to acknowledge my lovely wife Shirley for assisting me and standing with me during the writing, editing, and proofreading of my memoirs. Collaborating on the Final Round-Round 16 has been a lengthy process, and Shirley helped me complete this labor of love. I will forever be grateful for her participation.

Next, I'd like to dedicate the contents of this book to the memory of my beautiful, sweet daughter, Cheryl Ann Lee. She left us much too soon.

A special acknowledgment to my son Robert W. Lee Jr. No matter how difficult the situation, I can always count on him to be right by my side.

I would like to thank my good friend and spiritual mentor, Reverend Gerald King. He gave me the confidence to share some of my accomplishments my disappointments with the world. Reverend King convinced me that many of the stories from my life are both inspiring and historical. His enthusiasm convinced me to initiate the penning of my memoirs. The secret to a successful memoir is a top-notch writer. One who is patient and able to gently extract the memories that had been tucked away long ago. This special lady is Lisa Maydwell. Not only did she write and edit The Final Round-Round 16, but she plans to share the story on the big screen soon. Without her input and direction, we would have struggled to complete this journey.

I must acknowledge the support that I received from my family my entire life. They believed in me by celebrating my achievements and comforting me during my time of disappointments.

Reverend Michael and Donald Thomas, I appreciate your encouragement during the writing process. You both reminded me to move forward and never look back.

To my wonderful siblings: Rose, Patricia, Constance, Brenda and my brother William Jr. who wanted only the best for me. They supported me and cheered me on as I pursued my dreams.

To this list, I would also like to add a couple of people who helped me to move forward through the trials and triumphs of life: Leo Kaplowitz, Charles Irwin, Gerald Krovatin and most of all Jersey Joe Walcott.

Robert W. Lee Sr.
Round 15 The Final Round

As I share my story The Final Round, I would like to acknowledge and dedicate this book of memoirs to my Lord and Savior Jesus Christ. I would like to thank God for permitting me to be the vessel to help people accomplish goals that they never thought were possible. During my life, I was able to open doors in some areas and close them in others so that some of our people had the chance at upward mobility in their chosen careers. This book is a compilation of memoirs various sundry thoughts that demonstrate pride, performance, and opportunity as opposed to obstacles. The Final Round will reinforce the notion that winners never quit, and quitters never win. As you read my story you will see how our organization began at point A and through perseverance, trust, and faith in our Heavenly Father, how we were able to make monumental strides in the world of boxing.

As a child, I was told that I had a special gift and I should always use it to benefit others. I pray that when the time comes and I am face to face with my creator I will hear the words, "Well done my good and faithful servant; well done."

Robert W. Lee Sr.

THE FINAL ROUND

Come over here son and lift your shirt and let Miss Mable look at that mark on your side. Miss Mable looked at my side and shouted, "Praise Jesus!" Mrs. Barnes looking confused asked, "What's the matter, Miss Mable?" "This boy has been kissed by an angel.", exclaimed Miss Mable. "Look, it's as plain as day, this boy gon' have good fortune all of his days," said Miss Mable. "Really Miss Mable? My Robert?" Mrs. Barnes said excitedly. "I's not saying he ain't gon' have trouble, but he will always come out smelling like a rose," said Miss Mable.

ROUND 1

THE WEIGH-IN

CHAPTER 1

My parents William Lee and Alma Barnes migrated with their families in the early 1920s to Newark, New Jersey. They were later married and moved to Fanwood, New Jersey and lived with my paternal grandmother and aunt. My father built our house on a stretch of land between Scotch Plains and Fanwood, land that was purchased by a Caucasian man whose last name was Kramer. He sold the plots of land to the "Colored" folks that migrated to New Jersey from Florida, many of who knew each other. The area was called Kramer Manor. The families would help each other build homes and dig artesian wells for the community. Those were the days of outhouses. There were about twenty-five homes in our small community. My father was a hard worker who took pride in knowing that his family would always have a roof over their head, decent clothing, and three hot meals per day. My mother stayed home and took care of the family. She was known for being an amazing cook and for taking care of not only our family but providing for distant relatives who passed through our town in search of bigger and better opportunities.

As a child, I spent quite a bit of time with my paternal grandmother who was a feisty woman who didn't take crap from anybody. She was married to a Spanish-American war veteran who succumbed to pneumonia while serving our country. My father was no more than three years old when his dad died and never had an opportunity to be with him at length. My maternal grandparents who lived in Newark always made sure that our family always had proper clothing and food during the winter months when construction work was slow. My grandparents were especially fond of my sister Rose probably because she was the oldest grandchild and the only girl. They made sure that Rose had everything that she needed growing up.

We would regularly take the bus to our grandparent's home in Newark to visit them. They lived on the first floor of a three-family house, and we could always count on some good eating when we visited. My grandfather was a construction worker and I still remember him walking up the street, after work, carrying his silver lunch box and my sister Rose running to greet him. He would have the biggest grin on his face when Rose would grab his lunchbox and walk with him to the house sharing the events of the day.

My grandfather would often brag to his friends about his granddaughter, who was as kind and loving, as she was beautiful. We had a great relationship with our grandparents, and we enjoyed spending time with them whenever we could.

My grandmother was diabetic which caused her insomnia, so when everyone else in the house was asleep, she would cook enough food to feed everybody in Newark. I would ask her why she cooked so much food. She explained to me that you never know who may stop by for a nice hot meal. In those days most people didn't have phones and would send a letter informing my grandparents that they would be coming to visit. With both of my grandparents being unable to read, Rose would read the letters to them.

The out of town guest would arrive (by train) carrying greasy shoeboxes that contained the remains of fried chicken from their journey because they couldn't afford the food on the train. By the time the guests would reach my grandparent's home they would be famished. Grandmother would have a spread laid out for her guests which included chicken, pork chops, mashed potatoes, string beans, and macaroni and cheese. She would also prepare at least two desserts, one being her famous sweet potato pie. The travelers would normally stay anywhere from a few days to a few weeks. They would eat well throughout their entire visit. Some compared their house to the Underground Railroad, a place where you could get a good meal, a warm place to sleep, and good ole' southern hospitality. My grandfather was sympathetic to the travelers because he knew they were in search of a better life. This is where I believe my desire to help those who are less fortunate came from.

CHAPTER 2

There was a shopping center on Prince Street between Springfield Avenue and West Kenney Street in Newark where many people did their grocery shopping. I often went with my grandmother when she would go shopping. My grandmother was known for haggling with the vendors and threatening to go to other vendors if the price wasn't lowered. We would go to the chicken stand where she would select a chicken, watch while its throat was slit, dip it in hot water, and pluck the feathers. My grandmother wouldn't flinch as the unlucky bird was prepped for our evening meal.

One day when we went to the market my grandmother said, "Son", which is what she called me, "we need to make a stop because I saw something the other night while you were taking a bath. I want Miss Mable to take a look at it." I had no idea what she was referring to, but I didn't protest. We made our way to a makeshift shack that was on the hill on Broom Street, a short distance from the other merchants. We approached a strange lady who was seated in a beautifully carved high-back chair. She had a colorful scarf tied around her head and she wore a long flowing white dress.

She was surrounded by tarot cards, candles, and something that looked like chicken bones. The strange lady greeted my grandmother and invited us to come closer. My grandmother asked Miss Mable to look at a mark that was on my side. I was nervous when my grandmother instructed me to stand next to Miss Mable, lift my shirt, and allow her to look at the mark. I didn't know what this lady was going to do to me, and I asked if I had to lift my shirt. She said, "its okay son, let her take a look." I reluctantly lifted my shirt. Miss Mable looked at my side and said, "Praise Jesus!" My grandmother asked Miss Mable if there was a problem. "This boy has been kissed by an angel. He will be blessed all of his days and the Lord will

4

watch over him," exclaimed Miss Mable. "Can this be true? My Robert?" my grandmother asked excitedly. "I's not saying he ain't gon' have trouble, but he will always come out smelling like a rose." said Miss Mable. My grandmother seemingly pleased with this assessment of my birthmark, happily paid Miss Mable and seemed to have a little more pep in her step as we walked away from the strange fortuneteller lady.

When we got out of earshot, I asked my grandmother to explain what Miss Mable had said about my birthmark. She told me that Miss Mable said that I have been blessed and that means that we all must be careful of what we do to you and for you. Many years later, I would think about some of the challenges of my life and think about Miss Mable's words. I would wonder if there was truly a fence of protection surrounding me that kept me from harm. I would remember her words, "He's gon' have trouble, but he will always come out smelling like a rose.

We always looked forward to our grandmother's visits. She had this shopping bag with a red and white striped leather design. The bag was always filled with surprises. She would have beautiful articles of clothing for Rose, and shirts and sweaters for my brother and me that we could wear to school and church. Rose always received special gifts from both sets of grandparents because she was the first grandchild.

When I started my first job as a caddy, my parents would take some of my money to purchase items for Rose. They would say, "You want your sister to look nice, don't you?" Although I wasn't excited to give up my meager wages, I knew that I too wanted my sister to look her best.

CHAPTER 3

My sister Rose, my brother William Jr, and I all attended school Four in the Burroughs of Fanwood, it went from kindergarten through sixth grade. Seventh through twelfth grade was located at Scotch Plains High School. My brother William and I were only a year and a half apart in age, and since there were no other boys our age in our neighborhood, we always played together. Baseballs, marbles, and exploring in the nearby woods were how we entertained ourselves. I remember taking my brother to school for an open house and he was so anxious to attend. I told him not to worry, that he would be there soon enough.

The families of Kramer Manor were a close-knit community who was isolated from the communities of Scotch Plains and Fanwood. It wasn't until I entered junior high that I started to meet and socialize with other African Americans from the northside of town. I was often recognized as being a leader on the playground and this led to me being elected class president in the seventh grade. My friends teased me relentlessly for being class president, and they tried unsuccessfully to get me to vacate the office.

I fulfilled my presidential duties during seventh grade but decided not to run for office again. I decided to focus on sports. My father taught us to value our education which is why I excelled in school. After a long day at work, my father would come home and check our schoolwork to make sure it was completed. My love of sports made me very competitive and this carried over into my studies. I was determined to be the best student in my class. I was always in the top five of my class.

There was a girl named Mattie Mae in my class, but she should have been in class with Rose, but she had been held back. She was jealous of my sister and often tormented her. Mattie Mae would say the only reason Rose looked so good was that her grandmother purchased her clothing.

Rose would never feed into the argument until it became inevitable. Mattie began telling people that she was going to beat my sister up for dressing so nice. One day while on my way to baseball practice Rose approached me and asked me to walk her home. I explained to her that I had practice after school. She explained that Mattie Mae and a group of girls were threatening to beat her up. I decided to skip practice and walk her home.

On the way home about six girls, including Mattie began following us and taunting Rose. I warned the girls to leave my sister alone, but they continued to hurl insults at her. When Rose could no longer tolerate the insults, she said she was going to fight Mattie. I asked her if she thought she could whoop her. Rose said she wasn't sure if she could, but she was willing to give it a try. Rose turned to face her tormentor who continued to run off at the mouth. Without warning, Rose pushed Mattie in the face, punched her, and knocked Mattie to the ground. Rose pummeled Mattie until she was bleeding like a stuck pig. Eventually, I pulled Rose off Mattie and told her it was time to go home. As we were walking away, another girl threatened Rose. I told her if she put a hand on my sister, I would hit her so hard that her ancestors would feel it. The girl quickly stepped aside and let us walk on by.

Mattie became an outcast at school once word spread that Rose, who never bothered anybody, had whooped her. Mattie Mae had the nerve to come to our house crying to our mother about how Rose had beat her up after school. My mother calmly told her to go home and get patched up. She said that she had talked to Rose, and in the future, they should avoid any contact with each other. Mattie Mae tucked her tail and went on home. After she left my mother and I laughed as I explained how Rose jumped on the girl quicker than a flea on a dog and whooped her good. My mother and I both said we didn't realize that Rose could fight. Rose became one of the most popular girls at school after news of the fight got out. Mattie Mae eventually quit school before graduating, but we would still run into her from time to time, but she never said another word to my sister Rose.

ROUND 2
BANTAM WEIGHT

CHAPTER 4

I loved to play sports. Baseball, football, basketball, and track, and I had been blessed to excel in nearly every sport. I played intramural baseball against students from other schools in the district. I was very competitive. There was a pitcher from a predominately Italian school named Don DiFrancesco, his teammates called him Zuna. Whenever we played against Zuna, his classmates would chant, "Zuna's gonna get you today." Their chanting would be like fuel to my fire, causing me to send the ball soaring at what seemed like a hundred miles per hour towards the stands. I would fly around the bases and wink at Zuna as I rounded third base. Zuna and I would laugh about my antics after the game.

We would also play against an all-Black school. The coach would warn us to watch ourselves because it was located on the rough side of town. We usually lost to this team because the boys were older and larger than we were. The students at the all-Black school would be amazed to see the nearly all-White students cheering for me. Even though we would lose, it made me feel important the way my classmates supported me.

CHAPTER 5

During my senior year in high school, there was an opening for a caddy at the Shackamaxon County Club in Scotch Plains. My classmates convinced me to apply for the position. I hesitated because I didn't know anything about golf, and I wasn't sure where the country club was located. One of my classmates offered to come to my house so that we could ride to Shackamaxon together on our bikes. The country club was located on the border of Scotch Plains and Westfield. I made such an impression on the owners that they gave me a trial run even though I didn't know how to caddy. The first golfer that I caddied for, gave me lessons on how to be a good caddy. He told me where to stand, when to walk, and how to move. By the time we reached the 18th hole, I knew exactly what I was doing. I was happy with the money that I made because I knew that I would be able to help my family and enable my mother to buy herself something special.

The country club hired me for the summer. Each time I caddied I made between two and four dollars. This was a lot of money for a high school student in the 1940s. My parents were proud of me for getting a job and contributing to the family. I was happy that I could make things a little easier in the Lee household.

I enjoyed working at Shackamaxon but there was a White boy who had nothing better to do than to pick on me. He was always in my face saying that he wanted to fight. I tried to avoid him, but he made it impossible. One day I had enough of him, and I obliged him with a fight. We went around and around hitting each other and slamming heads to the ground. I was determined that this White boy wasn't going to whoop me. After about fifteen minutes of fighting, we both fell to the ground exhausted. He eventually went on his way and I continued to do my job. The very next day, the same White boy was waiting to fight me again because his buddies teased him for losing the fight. Reluctantly, I fought him again only this time I made sure that he wouldn't come back for more. The next time I saw him we struck up a conversation and realized that we had a lot in common. We became friends. He ended up becoming a noted cardiologist surgeon in New York.

When I wasn't playing sports, I was at the clubhouse working. An assistant at Shackamaxon named Danny took a liking to me and kept me busy doing various tasks around the golf course. He nicknamed me Rabbit. Danny would steer me toward the customers who gave large tips. I would take the money home to my mother and she would show her appreciation by preparing my favorite meal. I was at the golf course every chance I got.

I graduated from high school in 1951. I along with Betty Nettingham, Rosa May Jones, Delores Wise were the only African Americans in the class of 81 students. It saddens me to know that I am the only one that is still alive in that group. On graduation night, all the Caucasian boys loaded their cars with beer and wine and drove to the shore. They didn't invite me along. I couldn't be too mad because I knew that I wouldn't be welcomed because of the hue of my skin. I remembered an old country boy said to me some years ago that if I couldn't find a way, make a way. That's what I did. I didn't allow the racist actions of others to define who I was or what I could do.

I continued working at the country club even when it changed ownership. The new owner put his son-in-law, Bud Carter, in charge. They asked me to continue my employment and I became Bud's, right-hand man. I fixed the boiler and cleaned up the greens and I received 70 dollars a week. I was happy to have been allowed to continue working at Shackamaxon.

During my employment at the Shackamaxon Golf Club in 1952, there was a PGA golf tournament being held. As I stood near the course's waterfall, I noticed a group of people following some golfers. I did a double-take when I recognized one of the men. It was the heavyweight champion, Joe Louis. I stared at the famous boxer before making my way over to him. I began yelling out "Joe Louis" until I got his attention. I will never forget that big white smile as he asked me how I was doing. I couldn't stop repeating his name, I was star-struck. He introduced me to Sugar Ray who laughed at how large my eyes got when I saw Louis. Joe Louis was pleased that I was familiar with him and his work in the boxing ring. I told Joe Louis that I never expected to see him at the event. He explained that he was sponsoring a man named Ted Rhodes from Nashville, Tennessee who was playing in the tournament.

Ted Rhodes learned the game of golf while caddying at Nashville's Belle Meade and Richland Country Clubs. Rhodes was recognized as the first professional African American golfer. Rhodes often had problems obtaining sponsorship because of his color, that's where Joe Louis came in. That's why Joe Louis and his party of four were following Rhodes. I got up my nerve to ask Joe Louis for his autograph. He asked me for a pen and paper. I told him that I would be right back. I scoured around the golf course until I found a pen and paper and excitedly returned to the foursome for what I felt was a once in a lifetime opportunity. Although the writing looked like chicken scratch, I was excited to get the champ's signature. I thanked him for the autograph and shook his hand. I couldn't wait to go to the snack bar to show the autograph to my friends and tell them I shook the hand of the heavyweight champion of the world.

My friends gathered around me when I told them about my encounter with Joe Louis. My friends told me how lucky I was to have met both Joe Louis and Sugar Ray. That was the highlight of my time at Shackamaxon. I never ran into Joe Louis again. I would sometimes run into Sugar Ray in Harlem. He would proudly ride around in his pink Cadillac usually dressed in an expensive suit. He was always cordial when I would run into him.

CHAPTER 6

I graduated on a Tuesday and started working full time on Wednesday. I arrived each day with my lunch bag in hand ready to get to work. My buddy Jessie Seabon and I worked together cutting the greens, raking sand traps, changing the location of the pins, and various other tasks that Bud assigned. We even helped rebuild the clubhouse that had burned down a few years before we started working at the golf course. I enjoyed my job at Shackamaxon not only was I doing a job that I enjoyed, but it also allowed me the opportunity to help with my family's finances. My only concern was what would I do during the winter months. Bud promised to keep me on during the winter months, but he would have to lay off a fellow worker named Frank McCoy who had recently become a new father. I didn't want McCoy to have the burden of looking for another job, so I volunteered to be laid off instead.

ROUND 3
STICK AND MOVE

CHAPTER 7

My brother William was about to graduate from high school and enter college on a partial scholarship to play basketball, baseball, and football at Ithaca College in New York. I knew that my family wouldn't be able to help William financially, so I was preparing to help support my brother as he headed to college. I knew the time had come for me to get a higher paying job, but the available jobs didn't appear to me.

One day while eating lunch at the golf course, perched upon a five-gallon gasoline can, I read an interview in Readers Digest about a successful businessman who had become a millionaire. The man said he would take a job, advance as far as he could within the company, and then move on to the next company. He would continue this pattern until he finally reached the level of success that he had envisioned. The secret to his success was to identify your goals and move forward; never backward. The businessman encouraged others to emulate his strategy to achieve their goals. Reading this article encouraged me to look in earnest for a new career.

A New York magazine advertised for life insurance sales agents with New York Life Insurance Company who offered a salary of 40-50,000 dollars per year. This was an attractive starting salary. I applied for the position and was interviewed by an African American man sympathetic to my cause. He said they were hiring salesmen and they were paying a base salary plus commission, which was determined by the number of policies sold. The man explained that I would have to pound the pavement to be successful. I wasn't sure if this was something that I wanted to do. I told him that I would let him know if I was interested. He explained that I would work the Harlem and Bedford Stuyvesant area which were Black neighborhoods. "As a rule, Black people don't buy life insurance." the man said. He said with good salesmanship I might be able to convince them that insurance is a necessary expense. I told him that I didn't consider myself a salesman, and I didn't see myself driving to New York every day to do something that I wasn't good at.

My father insisted that I could learn how to be a good salesman and I should take a few days before I made a final decision. I did what my father said, but after a few days, I called the man back and declined the position. The man said he understood, and he told me if I ever needed anything to feel free to contact him. I thanked him, thought about the Readers Digest article and set my sights on bigger and better opportunities. For the time being, I would continue working on the golf course.

CHAPTER 8

The owner of Gehrig Products who played golf at Shackamaxon Country Club mentioned one day that he was hiring. He asked me if anyone at the golf course needed a job. I applied to Gehrig Products and was hired the next day. My father didn't believe that I was going to give up my position at Shackamaxon, but he understood my motivation.

For the second time since I began working at the country club, it was changing owners. Bud Carter took a position in Nyack, New York, eighty miles away from home. He was managing a different golf course. Carter asked Jessie and I if we were interested in coming to Nyack to work with him. We both accepted the offer. I took advantage of the two weeks of shut down that Gehrig Products had each summer to go work for Bud in Nyack. Jessie and I shared a large room in the beautiful clubhouse. Although I enjoyed working at the golf course, it was too far away from my family, and the people in New York weren't very sociable. If you weren't a native to the area, they gave you the cold shoulder.

I returned to Gehrig two weeks after their shut down had ended. The owner said that he'd missed me and asked me if I wanted my job back. I said that I did. I was grateful that the owner was so forgiving and gave me another chance.

CHAPTER 9

Shady Rest, in Scotch Plains, New Jersey was one of the few Black-owned golf courses in the United States. It was owned by William Willis, his sons Billy and Dewitt, and his nephew Jefferson Craig. Shady Rest had a bar, dance floor, and great musicians who played regularly. Count Basie, Duke Ellington, Jimmy Lunceford, and Cab Calloway all performed there.

One day while sitting at the bar sipping on a soda, I didn't drink alcohol. Billy Willis sat next to me and asked me my age. I told him I was 21 years old. He informed me the city of Scotch Plains was searching for a Black police officer. Billy mentioned that the legal assistant for the town council, Ursula Plinton, was searching for potential candidates. I knew Ms. Plinton because she played golf at Shady Rest. Her family was well known throughout New Jersey not only for her position on the council but also because her dad was a successful dentist and her brother a well-known mortician. Billy suggested that I apply for the position if I was interested.

As luck would have it, one day while driving my mother to Plainfield, New Jersey, I saw Ursula walking across the street. I jumped out of the car and caught up to her and asked her about the job on the police force. She asked if I had ever been in trouble with the law. I told her my record was squeaky clean and gave her my contact information, asking to be considered for the position. She said that she would contact me when she had more information.

A week later when I came home from a long night on the town with some of my buddies, I planned to sleep in. My sister came into my room yelling for me to get up. Reverend Glover and Deacon Boykin from the St. John Baptist Church in Scotch Plains, were downstairs waiting to speak with me. I stumbled downstairs in my robe, half asleep. Reverend Glover told me Scotch Plains was looking for a Black police officer and I was highly recommended. They wanted to know if I was interested. They discussed the potential salary and benefits that came with the position. Deacon Boykin warned me not to have relations with Caucasian women if I applied for the job. He said that they tend to gravitate toward men in uniform, and that can only mean trouble for a Black man. I told them that they didn't have to concern themselves with that. My mother taught me a long time ago Caucasian women were "rope poison" and to avoid them at all costs. My mother said there were plenty of Black women around. There were times that I didn't heed my parent's warnings, but on this particular subject, I listened. I was always focused on my education and sports...girls were the furthest thing from my mind.

CHAPTER 10

Reverend Glover submitted my name to the council for the position. He reminded me that if I were to get the job, I would have to work twice as hard as my Caucasian coworkers. He said, just know that you will always be watched. They will always look for you to stumble. He reminded me of how Jackie Robinson was expected to be better than all the other players to succeed. I explained that I was the man for the job, and confident that I would be able to handle the responsibilities and the scrutiny of the position.

The Republican City Committee reached out to set up a meeting at one of the member's home. I had to take a day off from my job at Gehrig to attend the meeting. I put on my best suit and arrived thirty minutes early. I was greeted at the door by members Davis Onque and Roy Kurre. The room was filled with committee members. Kurre introduced me to each member. The meeting was called to order and began with the question and answer portion of the meeting. They asked me about my educational background, my family, and my work history. They asked if I was registered to vote, which I wasn't at the time, so they instructed me to do so as soon as possible. I was also told that I would have to register as a republican. I told them that it wouldn't be a problem because I could see the bigger picture. They said they intended to hire me as a patrolman, but first, they had to get permission from the Scotch Plains Township Council.

I received a call a few days later asking me to attend the township council meeting. Upon my arrival, it was apparent that this was a closed session because I was the only non-member in attendance besides the Chief of Police. The council members began with another question and answer period. They asked me why I wanted to be a police officer if I had ever been in trouble with the law, and a few other details of my life. Once they were satisfied with my answers, they said my name would go on the shortlist for the patrolman position. I realized the police chief was looking at me like he knew me. Suddenly he approached me and said that he recognized me from playing baseball with his son Harry Haskell. He said his son always spoke highly of me. He walked over and shook my hand and abruptly left the meeting.

The council member who appeared to be in charge told me I was free to leave, and they would contact me when a decision was made. I continued working at Gehrig Productions while waiting to hear back from the City Council.

ROUND 4
OUTSIDE FIGHTER

CHAPTER 11

The following spring, I received a call from Davis Onque asking for my help to get candidate Mauro Checchio elected to the township council. I was flattered by the request hoping it was a path to the patrolman position. I attended a fundraiser where Mauro Checchio was the keynote speaker. He called to me from across the room. "Is that you Lee?" Checchio asked. He said they were thinking about doing something good for me. He mentioned that he knew the guys in the Jerseyland section of Scotch Plains. This alerted me that he didn't know who I was because I didn't live in the Jerseyland area. This made me wonder if Checchio was a sincere man and would he be an asset to the people in Scotch Plains. I had no problem doing what needed to be done as long as it had a positive outcome for my community. I shared this encounter with Ursula and in turn, she admonished the township council regarding their candidate's lectures to the community. Checchio was chastised for his lack of professionalism.

I was asked to set up coffee klatches around the city to help garner support for Checchio. I also used this as an opportunity to increase my chances of landing the patrolman position. Checchio attended one of the klatches and showed that he was a seasoned politician and great speaker. He spoke for what seemed like hours. The questions from the attendees focused on what Checchio was going to do for the community. He made the "Jerseyland", comment again and the crowd began to disperse realizing Checchio was just another politician who they would never see again once he got their vote. They believed that he didn't have their best interest at heart.

A pre-election party was held for the republican candidates and Ursula suggested that I attend the event. She promised to save me a seat at her table. This is when I met Bud Simmons, a candidate running for the assembly, and the only African American at that time to ever run for that position. He was a sharp politician but wasn't able to stem the "White tide", so he lost his bid for the office. However, he gained the respect of the party, made numerous connections, and received favors from those in the Republican party.

Several people in attendance at the pre-election party asked who I would be voting for. I told them Maurio Checchio. Many people agreed with me because he had won the 1955 councilman position by a landslide. This gained me favor with him and he told me that he would make sure that I got the patrolman's job.

Election day came and it was time to get the people to the polls. Davis Onque was scheduled to take people to the polls, but his wife died unexpectanly. The township clerk Helen Reidy contacted me to ask if I would be able to transport people to the polls. I drove numerous people to the polling locations, and they took note that it was the Republican party who got them there.

In January of 1956, while I was still employed at Gehrig, Mauro Checchio had been selected by his peers to be the mayor of Scotch Plains. In September of 1956, Mayor Checchio appointed me and three other people to be patrolmen of the Scotch Plains police department.

I received a call that the council was having a meeting and I was invited to attend. Upon entering the council meeting I saw three men who I didn't recognize as being a part of the council. One was a classmate from high school, another graduated with my brother, and I didn't know the third man. The council members informed us that we would all be appointed to the police department. We were assigned badge numbers 5, 6,7, and8. Of course, I received lucky number 7. We were sworn in and told to report to the police chief the next morning to complete the paperwork and receive our assignments.

CHAPTER 12

When we reported to the police chief the next day, we were told that we would be going to Newark, New Jersey to get our uniforms. As we were preparing to leave, a patrolman who I knew, pulled me to the side. He told me to pay attention to the chief because he was known for testing each recruit to see if they pay attention to details such as the color of a shirt in a store window or a license plate number. I told him that I appreciated the information and I caught up to the chief and the recruits and we headed to Newark.

The chief was always at least two steps ahead of us when we arrived. As we walked down Broad Street, I made sure to pay attention to everything around me remembering the advice that I had received earlier. As we walked the chief stopped suddenly and asked for the color of the tie in the store window. The other recruits looked around confused, and I answered that the tie was red. The second time the chief asked for the license plate number on the green car that we just passed. I was the only one able to answer the question. The chief, impressed by my attention to detail, said he knew that I was going to make a good officer. I was thankful for the heads up that I had been given on what to expect during this outing.

The owner of the shop where we would get our uniforms was a friendly guy by the name of Lee Shulman. He instantly took to me when he discovered that my last name was Lee. Shulman gave me extra attention making sure that I had everything I needed. He told me to be sure to call him if I ever needed help with anything. I assured him that I would, and from that day we developed a lifelong friendship.

We started our assignments the following week working the 8 am-4 pm shift. I was partnered with a man named Joe Powers who was given the task of showing me the ropes. I liked Powers because he was thorough with his duties and cordial to me. At the end of our shift on my first day, I asked Joe if that was all that we had to do. Joe replied that they were finished for the day. He laughed when I asked him if we had to empty wastepaper baskets and take out the trash. He told me those were the duties of the janitorial staff, not police officers.

That evening while walking home through Scotch Plains to Fanwood I was floating on air. I couldn't believe my good fortune of landing the position in the police department. As I walked home the people in my community cheerfully greeted me, and this made me feel like an important member of the community. The next day I was issued a gun from the police department. That's when I felt official. I couldn't believe it that I Robert W. Lee was a police officer in the state of New Jersey. It got even better when Joe told me that I would no longer have to walk home from work. They would have an officer drive me home each day. I knew that this would be a positive experience that would forever change the course of my life.

CHAPTER 13

My family and the people in my neighborhood were so proud to have me in the police department. The children in my community were proud to see an African American patrolman. I knew I had to be a positive role model for them.

I have always been a fast learner, so when our duties were explained, I caught on quickly. While being responsible for the entire township of Scotch Plains I took interest in my neighborhood of Kramer Manor and Jersey land which had about 200 homes. I was familiar with many people in both communities from my days of playing sports and hanging out with friends. When certain situations occurred, I preferred to be the responding officer, I knew that many of the Caucasian officers would approach the situation differently than I would with it being a Black neighborhood. Citizens in the community knew who the people were who didn't pay attention to their family's needs. I was cautious not to take away any chance the perpetrators had to live up to their familial responsibilities. I always thought there was a better way to handle the situation. I would use my investigating skills to try and resolve the issues by calling for a truce and to work on resolutions that would benefit the entire family. I would try to avoid giving jail time. Although I tried to bring peace to domestic issues, I had no problem sending hardened criminals to jail.

One incident that comes to mind is when I received a call of a car fire near Kramer Manor. When I arrived the crowd immediately called for the arrest of the suspected arsonist. Everyone pointed to a man leaning on a car nearby. As the firefighters extinguished the flames, I approached the man and asked his name. He said he was known as Big Poppa. I asked him if he set the car on fire and he replied that he had. He said he bought the car for his lady friend, but she wouldn't act right. I asked Big Poppa if she was his wife, and he said no, his wife was at home. He said his lady friend made him mad, so he set her car on fire. I told him that he couldn't go around setting fire to cars just because he purchased it, and someone wasn't acting a certain way. I informed him that it was considered arson. Big Poppa stated that he was just a po' boy who was a long way from home, and he didn't intend to cause his lady friend any harm. He went on to say that he was a deacon in the church, which I found ironic. Here he was a married deacon in the church flaunting the fact that he had a mistress. He said he didn't live in the area and had only come to Kramer Manor to see his lady friend. He said that there was no need to arrest him. I said there was a reason to arrest him, but I would compromise with him. I asked him to follow me to the police station so that his church members wouldn't see him get arrested for torching the car. I was trying to protect his reputation.

When we arrived at the station the police sergeant asked if I wanted to lock Big Poppa up. I said no. I then took him into the hallway and grabbed him by the shoulders and explained that the sergeant was letting me handle the situation. I told him to leave his lady friend alone or next time there would be no conversation, only bars slamming behind him. I told him I was sure that he didn't want word of this incident to reach his congregation, so it would be best for him to return home and leave all of this behind him. Big Poppa was grateful that he wasn't going to jail and assured me that he wasn't a bad guy. I saw him a few months later and he let me know that everything was going well.

The sergeant was satisfied with the way I handled the situation and would often ask me what happened to the guy who set the car on fire. This was an example of how I helped people avoid jail time and avoided destroying their lives.

CHAPTER 14

Another experience was when a Caucasian officer and I were sent to check on a man named John. I knocked on the door of his home and was told to enter. Walking into the house I spotted a small man pacing the floor. His wife and two sons were huddled in a corner. I asked them if they were okay, and then I asked John why the call was made. His wife said that her husband had a gun and was threatening to kill all three of them. I asked John if this was true. He kept repeating that they were messing with him. I told him that it didn't appear to be true since his family was cowering in a corner. I asked for the gun. His wife said the gun was in the coal bin. I asked his wife what precipitated this situation. She stated that John had a woman on the other side of town and continuously gave her his paycheck every time he got paid. She said this was taking away money from the household, and whatever he had left he would spend on liquor.

The Caucasian officer stood dumbfounded unsure of what to do. I instructed him to return to the car and I would handle the situation. I'm sure he was glad to exit this dysfunctional situation especially since it involved Black folks. When the other officer left, I asked John's wife if he was drunk. She said he was always drunk. I took the handgun from him, removed the bullets, and gave the gun to his wife.

I took John to his room and ordered him to get some sleep. I told him if I had to return to his house he was going to jail, but first I would beat his ass. I told him not to get out of the bed unless he had to pee. I told his family if they had any more problems to call the desk sergeant and ask for Bob Lee. I knew John had employees who relied on him for a paycheck, I didn't want to sacrifice their livelihood for his foolishness. It was plain to me, if the Caucasian officer had to handle the situation, John would be behind bars.

I encouraged people to work things out behind closed doors so the law wouldn't need to get involved. I was known in the community for being fair when it came to enforcing the law, that's what made people gravitate toward me.

The weekends at the Shady Rest golf course were always full of party-goers on the weekend. Around two in the morning we could count on receiving a call that a fight had broken out, it never failed. The Caucasian officers would lock up the fighters. I would break them up, tell them to sober up, and send them home. There were a few guys that would give me a hard time, but most of the African Americans treated me with respect.

ROUND 5

MAJOR DECISION

CHAPTER 15

Just as I was settling into my role as a policeman, I got the call from Uncle Sam that I had been drafted. It was November 1956 and I had been on the force for two short months. My orders were to report to Fort Dix, New Jersey on November 30, 1956. I was transported by the troop train to Fort Benning, Georgia to complete my basic training. This was my first time traveling that deep into the south. What an experience that turned out to be.

Upon my arrival in Georgia, the captain, who was Caucasian, gave the other recruits and me a lesson on how things worked in the south. He explained that it was a different kettle of fish than what we were used to. He said that many places in Georgia were still segregated and the laws were applied differently depending on the color of your skin. He also let us know that the local police had jurisdiction over the military. We were warned to watch what we said and where we ventured off to. This was a departure from what I was used to in New Jersey, but I was determined to have a successful military career. The Sergeant Major appreciated my attitude and hard work, so he made me a squad leader. I would be supervising ten men.

Shortly after arriving in Georgia I received a vaccine that made me very ill. The higher-ups thought I was faking my illness to get out of fulfilling my duties. It wasn't until my arm doubled in size that they finally paid attention to me. My arm also had an open sore that wouldn't heal, and it became infected. I was sent to the medic where I was given two aspirin and told to stay in the barracks for two days.

While confined, my meals were delivered to me, and I was ordered to get some rest. After a few days, the swelling finally went down, and I was able to return to my duties. I was informed that the smallpox vaccine caused my illness, partially because I had never had smallpox.

My first encounter with segregation was riding on the bus when we would go to town. The Black men had to sit in the back of the bus. It was at that moment I knew I wasn't going to like Georgia

CHAPTER 16

One Saturday while I was relaxing in my barracks, another soldier asked me if I knew how to golf. When I told him that I did, he invited me to play. He said it was a good way to get some exercise. The guy was surprised at my skills on the golf course. When we returned to the pro shop, the manager said he heard I was a pretty good golfer. He offered me a manager position in the pro shop. I asked him what the job consisted of. He said that I would oversee the pro shop and I would have the freedom to do whatever I wanted during my stay. It took two seconds to decide. I told him that I wasn't interested because I wanted to get out of Georgia as soon as possible. I explained that I didn't like Fort Benning and there was no way that I was going to spend an extra two years in Georgia. The manager insisted that it would be the easiest two years of my life. Playing golf whenever I wanted and getting paid to do it. I told him that the offer was tempting but I wanted to go home to my family, He said the job was mine if I changed my mind. I told him "No way, Jose." I completed my last eight weeks of training on the other side of Fort Benning, known as Sam Hill.

When I went to Columbus, Georgia I met a Black officer named Hickey. He was known as being tough on the men in the military and was known as a one-man police force. Hickey's girlfriend worked at the local movie theater and he would pick her up after her shift. As the story goes, a couple of men from the base who were tired of Hickey's antics stole a hand grenade with plans to throw it into Hickey's car while he waited for his girlfriend to get off work. The two enlisted men pulled up to Hickey's car. The man on the passenger side pulled the pin on the hand grenade and attempted to throw it into Hickey's car. The problem with the plan is Hickey's window was closed and the hand grenade fell to the ground. Hickey's car blew up, but he wasn't harmed. While Hickey vowed to find the culprits, the two enlisted men were never caught.

CHAPTER 17

After completing my time at Fort Benning, I flew for the first time to McGuire air force Base in New Jersey. I was holding on to the vomit bag because I almost got sick on the flight. I was fortunate to get on a plane because some of the men had to return on the troop train that I had formerly ridden. The train was disgusting, it reeked of body odor.

When I arrived at McGuire, we immediately went to Fort Dix, where we were informed that we would be shipping off to Germany in a few days. I decided that I was going to go home to see my family while I had a chance. A man who lived in a small town near my home offered to give me a ride. He dropped me off about a quarter-mile from my home. I was as thrilled to see my family as they were to see me.

The first thing I asked my mom to prepare for me was some of her delicious ho cakes that I would drench in Alga syrup. I filled my family in on my experiences in the army as I filled my belly with my mother's great cooking. After a few days of basking in the love from my family, I received a call from one of my military buddies saying that I needed to return immediately. He said they were about to start AWOL procedures against me. I tried to explain that I needed to spend time with my family, but he told me that they were about to pursue charges against me and throw me in the stockade.

My brother drove me back to the base. The African American officer that I had to report to upon my return wanted to know where in the hell I had been. I explained that the sixteen weeks away from my family had me missing my family and my mother's good home cooking, and I wanted to return home before heading to Germany. He told me he didn't know if I would be able to go to Germany because my name wasn't on the list. He said he didn't know if there was anything that he could do to get me on the list. The officer began walking around scratching his head repeating that he didn't know how he could help me. I told him that I had six dollars to my name, and I would be glad to give it to him if it would get me on the plane. The officer told me to give him the six dollars and he would get me on the plane. It was then that I realized I had been hustled for my last six dollars, but my name was added to the list to go to Germany.

Fortunately, in the army, you can survive without money because they provide food and shelter. It was a good thing because I was heading to another continent without a dime in my pocket.

When I arrived in Germany, I met a guy named Walker. He knew that I was a recruit and wanted to make sure everything was okay with me. I told him that I had just arrived, and I didn't have a dime to my name. He took me to the PX and bought me a sandwich. I felt like a million dollars because I was finally getting some food in my belly.

I was sent from Frankfort to Baumholder on a bus. Upon my arrival, I was asked if I had any typing experience. I was forewarned not to volunteer for anything, but I ignored the advice and stepped forward. Two other soldiers, Henry Lee and Ron Lewis also volunteered for clerical duty. I said that I could type 40 wpm, so they assigned me to headquarters battalion. I was the highest ranking in the battalion. Henry was assigned to A-Battery and Ron to C-Battery. I believe the sergeant major being a northerner and more tolerant of minorities was the reason he assigned me to headquarters to work closely with him. I was glad the good Lord had again granted me favor. Henry and Ron got the worst end of the deal because they had to deal with racist sergeants.

Another soldier, MacMuller, trained me on regulations and other information that I needed for the position. With my ability to learn quickly, I had no problem following MacMuller's instruction. The biggest challenge I had was getting acclimated to the typewriter because I exaggerated the extent of my typing abilities. I worked so hard in headquarters that I was told to slow down. I was making everyone else look bad.

I thought you said Lee could type 40wpm Sergeant Major said to Harold Ware. Ware replied that is what he was told. Ware pulled me to the side and told me what the Sergeant Major said and told me that I needed to improve the speed of my typing. I began going to the office to practice typing and eventually improved my speed. Two months passed and Sergeant Major approached me saying that I may not be the best soldier, but I was the best clerk he had. After a while, not only was Sergeant Major utilizing my services, the colonel and the captain had me doing their clerical work too. They expressed how lucky they were to have me on their team and showed their gratitude by excluding me from KP and guard duty. I was happy that I didn't have to get up in the middle of the night to perform guard duty. Once the troops were sent to Graplinwore and Vilseck where they calibrated the 2mm cannons, I was told that I had to join them. I wasn't thrilled about this because that meant I would have to sleep in the fields. I protested but was told it would be a good experience for me. When I arrived, dreading having to sleep outdoors, I realized they had set up an office in one of the long buildings. While the other men were calibrating weapons and running around the fields, I was sitting in the office doing clerical work for Sergeant major, the colonel, and the captain.

CHAPTER 18

I was walking around the base when Henry Lee, another battery clerk, asked me if I wanted to join him for some tee time on the golf course. At the first tee, we ran into the captain for the A-Battery and the chaplain. They asked us to join them. The chaplain was known for being an experienced golfer. Henry leaned over and whispered to me asking if I thought I could beat him. With a grin on my face, I told him to watch me work.

I hit the ball straight up the middle, so far that they all looked at me like I was from outer space. The chaplain said that obviously, I had played the game before. I responded that I had played a time or two in the past. I went on to play the best round of golf that I ever played in my life. It was like the ball had eyes because it would drop right into the hole. Looking back, I believe on that day I could have beat Tiger Woods. The captain blurted out that I was good enough to join the PGA tour, but we both knew the PGA during that time didn't allow Black people into their tournaments. That was the last time that I played golf with the captain and the chaplain. I guess it was due to the story circulating that Henry and I had soundly beaten two of the officers. Once Chef Solomon Alfred got wind of the match, he told anyone who would listen how the young recruit defeated the captain and the chaplain.

I competed in several tournaments on the base until they banned me from participating because I won four in a row and they wanted to give other golfers a chance. When I left the military, I tried to take my four trophies home, but customs wouldn't allow it. I asked them to give the trophies to some of the local children.

I spent two years in the military and just before I left was elevated to the 42nd field Artillery Group, a step up from the battalion. My boss,

Lieutenant Colonel Fox marveled at the way I worked. He was known for running a tight ship. He showed his appreciation by bringing me lunch and other small gestures just to say thank you

The Chief Warrant Officer position was offered to me, but I knew if I accepted it, I would have to reenlist for another six years, which was out of the question. I was anxious to return to my family. They tried in vain to explain the benefits that came along with the position, but I wouldn't budge. I had done my time. I was grateful for my time in the military because it taught me how to work with a variety of people and allowed me to travel to different countries. However, I was ready to go back to Scotch Plains, New Jersey and spend time with my family.

ROUND 6
NEUTRAL CORNER

CHAPTER 19

When I returned home, I helped my parents out around the house. I ran into the police chief, and he asked if I was ready to return to my position in the police department. I told him I planned to return at the beginning of the year. I wanted to relax for a couple of months. He said he understood since I had been in the military for two years and he would await my return in January of 1959. I went to sign up for unemployment to help me financially until the new year. Typically, the staff at unemployment agencies are known for demeaning those coming in for assistance, but I met a gentleman in the office that shut the door on that stereotype. The gentleman explained that I didn't qualify for unemployment because I still had leave time available from the military. That information certainly put a wrench in my plans.

I went to see the chief of police and explain that although my original plan was to return to the police force at the beginning of the year, my finances told a different story. The chief welcomed me back and instructed me to return to Lee's Tailor shop in Newark to be fitted for my winter garments. He offered to let me use a special police coat until mine was ready. I was ecstatic to get my job back especially with Christmas just around the corner. Upon my return to the force, I was able to purchase a car and I had money in my pocket. I fell right back into the groove of being a police officer as though I had never left.

I remained on the force from 1956-1965, but with the proverbial glass ceiling continuously bumping me in the head I knew that it was time to go. I applied for a vacancy in the prosecutor's office, because they never called me for the police sergeant's exam. I believed it was because they knew I would outscore the other recruits, which would have made me the first Black sergeant.

A candidate for a detective position, who had made a newsworthy arrest and was familiar with the responsibilities of being a detective was promoted to the position. My coworkers were surprised when I wasn't offered the job. That's when I enrolled in John J. College in New York and Fairly Dickerson University for public and policeman administration. I recalled Pastor Glover saying "Robert, you have to be better than them." so I challenged myself to be better. I told myself that I may not be first, but I definitely would not be last.

CHAPTER 20

Once I was snubbed for the detective promotion, I decided it was time to pursue a different career path. I consulted with Ursula Plinton and Davis Onque about leaving the department and possibly going to work for the prosecutor's office. They went to the prosecutor's office to meet with Leo Kaplowitz, the county prosecutor and asked him to add me to his staff. I was hired immediately. The police chief was livid when he heard that I was leaving. He said he didn't know why I was doing this. He felt like I should have remained on the police force until I retired. He didn't realize that I'd had enough of being out in the rain, snow, and the hot sun. I was ready to move on to something better. I knew the good Lord was grooming me for greatness. Joining the prosecutor's office was one of the best moves that I had made for my career. I took a leave of absence from the police department to join the prosecutor's office.

I was placed in an office with homicide detective Ed Pieterzak. On my first day in the office, he told me to grab my coat because we had to go to the morgue with the chief. We had to get the results of an autopsy performed on a murder victim. We arrived at the Sakowicz Funeral Home in downtown Elizabeth, New Jersey where I was introduced as a new investigator. I followed the lead of the chief and began taking notes during the procedure. Pieterzak was squeamish around dead bodies, which I thought was ironic. He excused himself from the room. I chuckled knowing the head of homicide couldn't stand to be in a room with a dead body.

After the autopsy, the chief invited Ed and me to lunch. I told Ed that I wasn't financially able to spend money at a restaurant. Ed told me not to worry, the chief would more than likely pick up the tab. I hoped so because the fifty cents in my pocket wasn't going to buy much of anything.

I breathed a sigh of relief when the chief reached for the check, I didn't know what I would have done if I had gotten stuck with the bill.

When we returned from lunch the chief went to the captain and told him that they had hired their new homicide detective. The captain confirmed it was me who they were discussing. The chief explained how I conducted myself at the autopsy. He said he wanted me to work closely with the medical examiner as part of my duties in the homicide department.

The next day I was informed that I would be on loan to the medical examiner's office for about three weeks because some politicians had fired the previous employee. My receptionist, Catherine B'Agostino told me what to expect in my new position. She explained that I would be the one to determine whether bodies would be sent for an autopsy or if they would be released to the family.

CHAPTER 21

One time that I had to make the decision was when I received a call from Plainfield, New Jersey about a dead baby. The cause of death was not apparent at the time. This case resonated with me because my daughter Cheryl was about the same age as the deceased baby. There was speculation on how the baby died, but in the end, it was determined that the baby's mother had rolled over on her during the night and smothered her. I kept thinking, what if this were my daughter.

The image of that baby being carved up during the autopsy did something to me that will stay with me for the rest of my life.

I had dual careers working for both the prosecutor's office and the medical examiner's office until I finally settled into the homicide department. I was sent to Cincinnati, Ohio along with Lieutenant Pieterzak for a week-long seminar at Kettering Institute.

There was a strangler who was terrorizing Cincinnati and while I was there a woman was found dumped in the river. Her autopsy was performed at Kettering. They realized the murder was committed by a copycat, so the serial killer was still on the lam. I returned to New Jersey soon after that, ready to continue my duties in homicide.

Pieterzak and I worked on many interesting cases including one that occurred September of 1966. I had just returned from a PBA convention in Atlantic City when the chief called the two of us into his office to fill us in on a double homicide on Nile Street in Elizabeth. When we arrived at the scene, cops were swarming everywhere. An older couple had been beaten to death by what everyone assumed was a robbery. The neighbors said they hadn't heard a thing due to heavy storms the previous night. The house had been ransacked, there were over seven-thousand dollars in bank wrapping bands, strewn across the floor.

We put out the word to anyone who had information about the perpetrators of the horrific crime to please come forward. We received some tips, but none of them panned out. As we looked around the house, we discovered additional money hidden in several locations. We found 8,000 dollars hidden in a chair and another 7,000 in a bag in their closet. The couple's daughter came to the house trying to gain access during the investigation but was turned away. The money was eventually turned in to the property room. I assumed their daughter was the beneficiary and claimed the cash.

I was given the caseload of child abuse cases that no one else wanted. They claimed it was due to how well I handled the Plainfield case. I began working with a group from the Bureau of Children Services. Whenever there was a case that needed special attention the workers would call me.

One case that stood out was the case where a man was accused of abusing his daughter in Elizabeth, New Jersey. The caseworker said the last time she confronted the father he tried to get physical with her. She felt that I could handle the situation better than she could. When I entered the apartment, I was greeted by a giant of a man who stood well over six feet tall and weighed over three hundred pounds. I prayed to the Lord that I wouldn't have to wrestle with that massive mound of flesh, but instead, he invited me into his home.

I explained that I was there to check on his daughter because there was a complaint against him. The man explained that he was trying to take care of his teenage daughter while his ailing wife was in the hospital. He said the teen was giving him fits. His daughter enters the room with a golf ball-sized knot on her head right between her eyes. I asked the girl how she got the knot on her head. She said her father hit her. I told him that he should be ashamed of himself. The man apologized and explained that he was very concerned about his wife, and his daughter was acting like a fool.

He began sobbing uncontrollably when the daughter began to detail the abuse. She said her dad wouldn't allow her to go to the hospital to see her mother, who was very sick. The girl said she was sneaking out of the house to go to the hospital to visit her mother. She said her father hit her and she called BCS to report it. I told the man if I had hit your daughter like that, you would have tried to beat me to death. I told him that I have a daughter and would never hit her upside her head like that. I asked him what did he think would happen if she went to school like that, or worse what do you think your wife will do if she saw that knot? The man began to beg his daughter for forgiveness. I instructed the girl to put some ice on her head to help with the swelling. By the time I left, they were hugging and apologizing to each other. I warned the man if I received another call of abuse that I would return with an army of cops ready to arrest him and throw him in the county jail. As I left, I was happy to have resolved the daddy/daughter issue without having to mess up my suit. I never heard from the family again.

Lieutenant Pieterzak and I worked over twenty-eight homicide cases and we got convictions on all of them. We had a great record when it came to catching criminals. We developed relationships with everyone in our city, including the homosexual community. They stayed together, hung out together, and when something went wrong, they were there for each other. African Americans in New Jersey seemed to have an overlying tension in the air, probably due to the mistreatment of so many of our people. African American's confrontations were often made public while Caucasians were more subtle. In the end, both were just as damaging.

ROUND 7

THE GLASS JAW

CHAPTER 22

My passion has always been to help others who are in need. I was committed to opening doors for others because people opened doors for me. I was the first African American in the homicide department and the prosecutor's office and I reached back and helped others get into the office. When I went to Hudson County as lieutenant of investigators there were four African Americans who worked for me. I was committed to the Civil Rights Movement and was glad the Lord put me in a position to reach back and help others that looked like me. I was in the position at Hudson County for exactly one year due to the blatant racism and favoritism. It was too much for me to deal with.

In 1971, I decided to run for sheriff in Union County, where I lived. I made history as the first Black man to run for the office. I knew the director of the Division of Consumer Affairs, who helped me get a job to sustain me while I campaigned. My initial position was a chief investigator and then I went on to be Deputy Director. I would work from nine to five at my regular job, and campaign for sheriff well into the evening. It was a great learning experience and running for sheriff opened a lot of doors for me.

It was during this time that I learned a few lessons about the political world that would forever resonate with me. One lesson was, popularity can overshadow ethnicity. People will either gravitate toward you or against you.

I spent many hours campaigning in areas with a high concentration of Black voters. My task was to get African Americans to support my bid for sheriff and to make their way to the polls. A fellow political candidate advised me on the counties to visit and which ones to avoid. He told me about an area that didn't like Italians, that I may be able to carry. He said because my last name is Lee, I had a chance. The only glitch was, I couldn't let them see me. They would vote for anyone who they perceived not to be Italian, except an African American. I had to be invisible in this community.

CHAPTER 23

A place politicians frequented was the Italian open-air market in Elizabeth. One Saturday morning several of my party members and I were shaking hands and chatting it up with the customers. The word was out that the governor, William T. Cahill, was scheduled to visit the market later that day. I was prepared for the moment wearing my best suit along with a proper hat. A few of my family members, including my mother, came to the market to join in the excitement of the governor's visit. Arnie Highsmith, the owner of the Savoy Club, was also in attendance. He expressed how great it would be to have the governor visit his club as a fundraiser for my campaign. I liked the idea but didn't think we would be able to get the governor to agree to it.

The crowd began to buzz saying Cahill was coming. He walked into the market in his fine suit, looking like a million bucks. He came in saying he wanted to see the sheriff. He said he wanted to see Bob Lee. I was surprised, I was the only person of color on the Republican ticket. My party members came to me saying the governor would like to have a word with me. When he saw me, he said it was great to finally meet me. I remember thinking to myself, how does this man know me.

Cahill explained that he had been flown in by a helicopter from Trenton to Scotch Plains. He received an escort to Elizabeth by a police officer named Johnny Powers. He asked me if I knew Powers because he talked about me the entire way here. I explained that Johnny and I had been partners at one time. The governor said Johnny told him what a great cop I had been and how I was an all-around great guy. He gave his word that he was going to do all that he could to make sure that I won the election. He enlisted congressman Beck Reynolds and one of the county sheriffs to assist with my election. The governor said If I was as great as everyone said, I would be an asset not only to the party but also for the people of Union County. I was glowing and grinning like a Cheshire cat. This man who I just met was singing my praises and it felt good. Arnie reminded me to ask the governor to visit the Savoy. I was hesitant to ask him to make a cameo appearance but then Governor Cahill asked if there was anything, he could do for me.

CHAPTER 24

Governor Cahill and his driver followed me to the Savoy Club. He promised that he would stay for a few minutes before heading to the city hall. Arnie went ahead of us so that he could gather a crowd to greet the governor. The first people that greeted the governor was my mother and my aunt Anne Williams, they both spoke to him like they were old friends. As the governor circulated the club, I noticed a group of men who refused to cross the street and enter the club. I brushed it off and went back inside.

The governor walked through the club grinning and shaking hands with the patrons. One guy leaned back in his chair addressing the governor as "baby" and asked when he planned to hire some Black people. The governor said that he already employed Black people and invited the man to come to his office and look around. The man said he just might take the governor up on his offer, then turned his attention back to the small television behind the bar.

Cahill thanked me for the invitation and departed for the city hall. When the governor left, I approached the men who were still standing across the street and asked why they refused to come into the Savoy. The men said they didn't come in because they thought it was a raid and they wanted no parts of it. One man said that when he saw the police car, he figured there was going to be trouble.

Even with the support of the governor of New Jersey, I lost the election by 20,000 votes. This was the closest anyone had come to defeating the incumbent. I was genuinely surprised that my people came out to support me, but I did poorly in communities with a heavy Italian population. I was the only republican that lost during the 1971 elections in Union County.

CHAPTER 25

It was time for the annual Governor's Ball which was held in Sea Girt, New Jersey in a large outdoor tent. There was music playing and a buffet with all the food that you could eat. There were over one thousand people in attendance, and they offered valet parking. I was fortunate enough to get two tickets from a coworker for this much-anticipated event. I was warned by the coworker to take a date with me, especially since it was a formal event. He explained that Caucasian men would accuse me of looking at their women. He said it would be best if they thought I was in a relationship. I took my girlfriend, Shirley, who later became my wife. We marveled at the beauty of the event. They truly spared no expense to put on the event.

When the governor spotted me, he came right over saying that he had been waiting on me to arrive. He announced to his guest that I ran for sheriff on the Republican ticket. I couldn't believe that I was surrounded by these rich and powerful people as I stand with twenty dollars in my pocket. I later learned the ticket price for this event was one thousand dollars per person. That amount of money could have fed my family for nearly a year.

The next event that my wife Shirley and I attended was a fundraiser for Vice President Spiro T. Agnew which was held at the armory in Westfield. We were invited by some of my political pals. They insisted that I meet the Vice President. Upon our arrival, Vice President Agnew hugged me and told me it was a pleasure to meet me. Although he didn't know me, he was showing respect to someone in the same political party.

I spotted several of the people who had helped finance my campaign during my bid for sheriff, many of them I hadn't seen since the election. Some of them were curious as to what my next endeavor would be. They offered their support and resources if I decided to run for the office again. Running for sheriff turned out to be very beneficial for me.

ROUND 8
RABBIT PUNCH

CHAPTER 26

I returned to my position at Consumer Affairs as the Acting Deputy Director. Later I became the acting director until they decided to go in a different direction with the office. Millicent Fenwick was hired as the director and I returned to my original position. A position opened at the Office of Consumer Affairs in the State Athletic Commission. They were in charge of boxing and wrestling. The governor appointed tennis great Althea Gibson to the position as a reward for her status in tennis. Ms. Gibson was not knowledgeable about boxing and wrestling, and she didn't have any experience with being a commissioner. I was assigned to assist her to learn the duties of the job. I traveled from Newark to Trenton each day to fulfill my assistant duties for Ms. Gibson.

Althea's manager was difficult to get along with. We butted heads daily. He was very arrogant. I had to constantly remind him that I didn't work for him. I was on loan from Newark and not a permanent fixture in the commissioner's office. The final straw with the manager came in 1976 when I was selected to be an alternate delegate at the Republican convention. It was the year President Ford ran against Ronald Reagan for president of the United States. The convention was held in Kansas City. I utilized some of my vacation time and went to the convention. When I returned, Althea's manager began to verbally assault me saying "Don't no niggers be Republican." I corrected him saying that first I wasn't a nigger and secondly, my ancestors died so that I could be whatever I wanted to be. I was furious and went to the director and told him that I could no longer work with that man. I stayed in the position for another year before departing.

In 1977 Althea Gibson resigned as the commissioner. Governor Brendon Byrne Walcott, a former heavyweight champion, to the commissioner position. Walcott's director was Adam Levin, whose family made a fortune building malls. They were looking for someone to help them run the office. Levin approached me to see if I was interested in being Walcott's assistant in the commissioner's office. Of course, I was excited for the opportunity to work with the former heavyweight champion whose career I had followed for years.

In 1978 I began my career in the State Athletic Commissioner's office working with the great Jersey Joe Walcott. As a teen, I had a brief stint in boxing, but this was my formal introduction into the world of boxing.

CHAPTER 27

As a teen in the summer of 1950, my brother and I would go to the gym to play basketball. There was an area for boxing in the gym and occasionally I would put on the gloves for a round or two. The boxing coach saw my skills in the ring and asked me to join the team, if my parents didn't object. I told him they didn't care what I did if I stayed out of trouble. My brother and I both joined the boxing team. Each day we would walk two miles to the gym to box and make the two-mile trek back home after sparring. In those days there were no cars to transport kids to their activities. If we wanted to go somewhere, we had to walk.

I remember an amateur boxing match that my brother and I attended in Plainfield. My brother lost his match. I recall the pain of watching my brother get beat up knowing there was nothing that I could do to help him. I was victorious in my match.

At the time I was also on the baseball team. I broke my finger during a baseball game that required surgery and I had to wear a splint. The surgery was performed on November 4, 1950, in Muhlenberg, Hospital. I remember the date because it was the same day of the assassination attempt on President Harry S. Truman on the steps of Blair House in Washington DC, by a Puerto Rican group seeking independence. Even though my finger never healed properly, I continued playing baseball. At the age of 86, that bump remains on my finger.

CHAPTER 28

Jersey Joe Walcott knew boxing, but being an administrator was a different animal. That's where I came in. My previous experience as a clerk in the military enabled me to help Joe. I helped with reading, writing reports, and anything else that needed to be done. My time working with Walcott was a positive experience because he was such a genuine person. We also became good friends.

CHAPTER 29

We finished our business in Florida and returned to New Jersey. Upon our return, I received a call from Bob Arum, a promoter with roots in the WBA, with news from the convention. He informed me that when we left the officials held an election and I was voted in as Second Vice President in absentia. The first vice president was a supreme court justice from South Africa. I was confused as to why they elected me. Bob Arum said it was probably in response to the protest that I made during the convention. He said the members wanted someone in office who had guts and drive, someone who couldn't be pushed around.

In 1982, after the WBA elected me second vice president, Rodrigo Sanchez fell ill with stomach cancer, and he began to delegate more responsibilities to me due to his failing health. Sanchez knew he would have caused an uproar if he tried to pass those duties to the first vice president, Judge H.W. Klopper from South Africa. People were still boycotting South Africa because of apartheid.

Sanchez was pleased with the work I was doing in his absence. He wanted to make sure that I was prepared to attend the convention with him in Ottawa Canada, which was being held in October of 1982. Sanchez was looking forward to attending the convention even though his prognosis was grim. Sadly, Rodrigo Sanchez died in the summer of 1982.

Judge H.W. Klopper ascended to the role of president of the WBA which didn't bode well with the Canadians. They refused to acknowledge him as the new president. The powers that be stepped forward and declared that if Klopper remained as the acting president, they would not recognize the WBA and would refuse to hold the convention in Canada. The WBA had to scramble for an alternate location to hold the convention. I suggested they move it to Atlantic City to the Resort International Hotel.

We received the okay from Frank Gelb, the New Jersey-based promoter who was a driving force behind promotions in Atlantic City.

They finally decided to hold the convention at the Dupont Plaza Hotel in San Juan, Puerto Rico. Gilberto Mendoza of Venezuela threw in his hat into the ring to run for the WBA president. I would oppose Mendoza in the bid for the presidency.

I had many supporters in my bid to become the president of the World Boxing Association. Many wanted the leadership of the organization to return to the United States after being in South America for nearly a decade. The promoters complained that there was a communication gap with the leaders of South America because of the difficulties of their antiquated phone and telegram system.

Robert W. Lee at his IBF/USBA office

CHAPTER 30

The stage was set for me to be elected as the next WBA president. The top supporters of the WBA were Jimmy Binns of Philadelphia, Nick Kerasiotis of Illinois, Chuck Davey of Michigan, and York Van Nixon of Washington DC. My team consisted of Butch Lewis of Delaware and Dan Duva from New Jersey. They both supported having an American at the helm of the WBA so that Americans could regain control of the organization. This would prevent American fighters from being disenfranchised due to South American's having control over the WBA.

The WBA executive officers decided to have the annual convention in October of 1982 in the Dupont Plaza Hotel in Puerto Rico, which blocked me from hosting it in Atlantic City. With the number of Latin Americans on the executive committee, they had controlled the agenda for several years. The presidency of the WBA hadn't been in the United States in over nine years and I was trying to bring it back. I felt that the American boxers deserved it because some of the best fighters in the world are from the United States and much of the money used to pay the fighters came from American casinos and television stations. My opposition was from Mendoza and Pepe Cordero, also known as the "Bag Man". They didn't want me to win the presidency.

CHAPTER 31

We sought out someone who spoke Spanish fluently to help us strategize to win the election. Two guys were recommended to me by a New Yorker named Chet Cummings. Cummings was known as a gadfly who traveled within the boxing community to stay on top of boxing news. He wanted to introduce me to the men because they were interested in getting a license in New Jersey. Cummings knew that as the Deputy Commissioner I was the one who could help them with their request. One of the men was Victor Quintana, a boxer, and the other was Reggie Barrett. These two men wanted to open an organization in New Jersey to promote boxing.

Joe Walcott had a policy on becoming a promoter in the state of New Jersey. You had to obtain three permits, which was a trial run. If they did well with the three permits, then he would consider issuing a license to promote. Quintana and Barrett filled out the forms and sent them in. After receiving the application and checking their backgrounds Walcott refused to issue them a license. Their office was located near Madison Square Garden in New York City, at least that's where they claimed it to be. They asked about the upcoming convention in Puerto Rico and said they wanted to support my campaign. I told them their support would help get our delegates to the convention to vote. Quintana and Barrett showed up to the convention and helped to plan my campaign. Quintana spoke the language, so he felt right at home. He eventually worked his way on to our team.

I often thought that someone from our camp was taking information back to Mendoza's people because they seemed to out-flank us on whatever we tried to do. So, I knew there was a leak inside our camp. We all had our suspicions, but we never figured out who the rat was.

ROUND 9
KIDNEY PUNCH

CHAPTER 32

The WBA convention had begun and the first person that I see in the lobby was Mendoza. We shook hands and wished each other good luck and then began lobbying for the presidency. I did well on the straw vote which unnerved the people from South America including Binns, Kerasiotis, Davey, and Van Nixon. People began arriving from the states, not because they had voting rights, but they had an interest in seeing me win.

Mendoza had supporters from Latin America, Europe, South Africa, and Japan. There were rumors that Mendoza was offering special favors to many of his supporters if he were victorious in the upcoming election.

The agenda during the beginning of the week was taking care of the usual business, the latter part of the week is when the elections were held. After the business meeting on Wednesday, the participants were free to go sightseeing or enjoy some free time. The officials rolled up their sleeves and discussed issues such as referee and judge placement, rendering the official reports, and expectations of the members of the organization. The meeting was chaired by President Judge Klopper and me. We sat at the dais while Mendoza lobbied the audience for votes.

CHAPTER 33

Around 7 pm Thursday evening Hawaiian delegate Bobby Lee, no relation, arrived at the hotel. They called him the Brown Bobby Lee and I was the Black Bobby Lee. Judge Klopper permitted Brown Bobby to take the podium. He asked if all business was concluded. Klopper said yes. Bobby Brown then called for the election of the officers to be held immediately, this caught everyone off guard. Another official stood up to second the motion. Bob Arum, who had been quiet up to that point, jumped up and yelled for Mike Mortimer of South Africa to close the meeting. Arum knew if the vote were to happen at that moment, Mendoza would lose the election. Arum reminded Mortimer that several of the delegates weren't in attendance. They were out enjoying the city. Mortimer ran over to Klopper and told him to declare the meeting over. Klopper banged the gavel and ended the meeting. Klopper's actions threw the crowd into a frenzy. My supporters shouted in protest across the room. I heard someone else shout "Do it now!" and another man yelled, "You can't do that." Lou Duva ran up to the podium and screamed that the election process had already been approved and could not be stopped. Looking around the room, I knew that if the vote were held, I would have won by at least ten votes.

CHAPTER 34

An attorney from Puerto Rico, Luis Salas, said Klopper could do whatever he wanted. Salas and Duva began shouting at each other, standing toe-to-toe ready to battle. Salas threatened to have Duva thrown in jail. People were shouting that the election had been called off, while others yelled to allow the vote to proceed. Many of Mendoza's people didn't know what was going on because most of the shouting was in English. The headsets couldn't keep up with the translations. After Klopper banged the gavel, he got up and walked away from the dais. His appointed officials followed him out of the room. I was left standing at the podium alone. Meeting adjourned.

CHAPTER 35

During the night Mendoza's American supporters went into action. They began contacting delegates who supported Mendoza and had voting power. The delegates began arriving, many without credentials to prove their ability to vote. The games had begun.

On the morning of the election, I was greeted in the hallway with a wave of yellow shirts that said: "Vote for Mendoza". I noticed that some of the delegates from the Dominican Republic and Japan who originally supported me were now donning the yellow shirts. I knew their votes would change the tide of the election. The voting machines were positioned on the hotel patio near the pool, across from the buffet. There were several members from Puerto Rico standing by the voting booth "strongly urging" delegates to vote for Mendoza. They were intimidating the delegates with knives from the buffet table. To members from some of the foreign countries, these acts were frightening.

CHAPTER 36

The level of intimidation surprised many of us. Butch Lewis, Don Hubbard, Dan Duva, Luis Salas, and I watched the charade unfold before our eyes. Several police officers were called in to stand by in case a disturbance took place after the election.

After the votes were tallied, Mendoza was victorious by a mere nine votes. The delegates who had jumped ship affected the outcome of the election. This process taught me a valuable lesson when it came to the game of politics. I shook hands with Mendoza and congratulated him on his win. I was asked to run for the first vice president. I declined. Mendoza's people tried to convince me to run. I told them I ran to be first; not second. During my concession speech, I vowed that this would be my last time attending a WBA event. I announced to the crowd that I was finished with all that nonsense.

ROUND 10
KISS THE CANVAS

CHAPTER 37

Jersey Joe tried to console me all the way home after the fiasco in Puerto Rico. He said that I took a shot at it and there was nothing else I could have done. Joe said that we can't forget the men who did us wrong, particularly the Americans. I told Joe that I wouldn't forget. Turnabout is fair play.

We started preparing to attend the annual United States Boxing Association convention at Resorts International Casino in Atlantic City in April of 1983. When we arrived all the delegates were in attendance from North America except for Kerasiotis, Davey, Binns, and Van Nixon. They never showed up for the mandatory meeting. Some of the guys in attendance said they too had been in Puerto Rico lobbying, sitting in on meetings, and voting for me to be the WBA president. They bought into the notion that the United States should be in control of one of the sanctioning bodies. The other sanctioning body was also a Latino organization, so Americans didn't stand a chance.

After the completion of the opening meeting at the convention, the discussion turned to my loss of the WBA presidency. They were livid about the way the elections were conducted. That's when the discussion of starting another organization with me as president began. One official said since I was already the president of the USBA and I had a better handle on boxing nationwide and worldwide, I could be the president of the new organization until there was an official election. We determined that all officers of the USBA would remain the same except for the ones that I would appoint.

The overwhelming consensus was we could do international boxing on our terms. We didn't need the other federations. I was asked if I would accept the offer to be the president.

CHAPTER 38

Bob Weitzel from Portland, Oregon said he was fed up with the other organizations because they didn't respect Americans. Weitzel said it was time to form an international organization, this was something we had talked about in the past. He said we could show them how it should be done. Weitzel then asked everyone in the room to raise their hands if they wanted me to be the president of the new international organization. Everyone raised their hands except for Arch Hindman of Ohio. He didn't want to be involved in a new international organization because he was a long-standing member of the WBA. He didn't want to choose between the two. Weitzel announced Me as the president of the new organization.

I pondered the offer for a moment. I didn't want to accept because I had been kicked around pretty good in Puerto Rico. My supporters told me I had to accept the offer. They said I owed it to the sport of boxing. I finally relented and accepted the presidency. I figured that down the line someone else would take over as the leader. I announced I would accept the position if it was under the USBA-I title, making it an international organization. We had an agreement that the current officers in the USBA would become the officers in the IBF (International Boxing Federation). I didn't want to reinvent the wheel, I only wanted it to run a little smoother. Hindman oversaw drafting a new set of rules to be added to the USBA booklet. The USBA rules would be in the front of the book and the USBA-I rules in the back. It was made official that I was the USBA-I president, and James Stevenson would be the commissioner. Everyone cheered as we celebrated our new business venture.

CHAPTER 39

Francis Walker, the executive secretary from Pennsylvania was nominated to be the Ratings Chairman of both organizations and Bill Brennan was nominated to be the Championship Chairman of both organizations. Walker said he would pull together the ratings so that we would be on even footing with the other federations so we could properly compete against them. He said he would distribute the ratings to the media and the other organizations so they would know who we are.

Unfortunately, Walker ran into some difficulty with his bosses at the Commonwealth of Pennsylvania. He was informed that he could no longer hold the position of ratings chairman with our organization. He relinquished his post and his position in the USBA-I. This sent me in search of a new ratings chairman.

Bill Brennan was the executive secretary for the state of Virginia, and he had several people working under him. Brennan suggested Doug Beavers, who he said was a hard worker, to join our organization. Brennan said that he planned to retire soon and was contemplating moving Beavers up to his position as executive secretary, and he would bring him on as our new ratings chairman. When Brennan sent me Beavers' credentials, he assured me that Doug Beavers was loyal and a dedicated worker. He said he would vouch for him 100%. Brennan suggested I try Beavers on a trial basis to see if he was a good fit for our business, and if I liked him, I could keep him on as our ratings chairman. It wasn't like I had much of a choice because Beavers was the only candidate for the position.

CHAPTER 40

Beavers turned out to be a good selection for the position because he was diligent with his duties. We would sit in his basement with multiple television sets, watch boxing matches, and rate fighters from all over the country. He was able to pick up some international channels and he would watch those fighters and properly rate them all. Beavers did a great job. He was quickly becoming the best ratings chairman in the sport of boxing. He would submit the information to me, even though I had limited knowledge of the rating process. I would compare his data to the other federations, boxing publications, and magazines. Beavers would be right in line with their stats. Many times, I thought he did a better job than the other sources.

An executive committee meeting was scheduled for July of 1983 in Reno Nevada. The press laughed when we notified them. They called us another alphabet organization and wanted to know our agenda. The press gave us the blues. Others were excited about the addition of another federation, saying it was a good move on our part. I always had faith and believed, "As long as I had the good Lord in front of me, in back of me, and I can reach out and touch both sides, I don't have to worry about what people say." "If the good Lord is for me then the world can do me no harm."

We reached out to the media, promoters, and various boxing journals informing them of our new organization and we asked for their support. We explained that the USBA-I was under the umbrella of the USBA, as they were under the same corporate structure. Our next course of business was to look for an office in Newark to set up shop.

Due to the unfair election in Puerto Rico, I received support from several states. They were offering to help in any way possible, to make the new federation a success. We let it be known that we were ready to compete with the other organizations on equal terms.

ROUND 11
NO DECISION

CHAPTER 41

When I arrived on the boxing scene in 1978 as the Deputy Commissioner, I had heard about boxing promoters Don King and Bob Arum. They were known as the premier promoters in boxing worldwide. New Jersey was not a state known for hosting main event boxing matches that would entice King and Arum to New Jersey. A short time later the Resort Hotel and Casino opened. They were interested in hosting professional boxing at their location. They were aware that people who came to the casino to gamble would also pay to see a boxing match. The first order of business was to change the New Jersey boxing rules to align with professional boxing rules. There had to be three-minute rounds with one round to rest. Jersey Joe also wanted to add a "knockdown" timekeeper on the sidelines along with professional referees and judges.

Initially, we weren't equipped to handle overseeing the boxing matches, so we recruited a couple of guys from New York who were licensed to officiate. One of the officials was Tony Perez. We also got a couple of guys who were successful in working in both New Jersey and New York. We were creating a powerful officiating team.

The first time the State Athletic Commission and I had business with King and Arum is when Philadelphia's Matthew Saad Muhammad, the WBC light heavyweight champion wanted to fight a boxer from England named John Conteh in a fifteen round fight August 18, 1979, in Atlantic City. This was the first world title fight that was hosted in New Jersey. Muhammad was a sharper puncher, but Conteh was a skilled boxer. He knew the ring well. We conducted the weigh-in and both boxers made weight. We worked with the WBC to appoint the officials, set up the weigh-in, and discuss all aspects of the rules.

Frank Gelb was the go-between for Bob Arum and the Casino Control Commission. The matchup was expected to be impressive, and the fight was being televised on ABC Wide World of Sports.

CHAPTER 42

As is customary, the referee went into the dressing rooms to let the fighters know what would be expected during the match. Muhammad's camp was concerned about Conteh's reputation for head-butting his opponents. They didn't want Conteh to reinjure a cut above Muhammad's eye. Ray Clark from England, a representative from the WBC, promised that they would be on alert for Conteh's unsportsmanlike behavior. Clark was from England and was aware of Conteh's reputation.

It was fight night and things were going smoothly until the sixth round. Conteh, up to his old tricks, head-butted Muhammad which reopened the wound above his left eye. Muhammad's renowned Cut Man, Adolpho Ritacco, went to work on the cut. He stopped the bleeding, then sent Muhammad back in. Muhammad went on to win the fight which brought out protests from Conteh's people. They were certain Ritacco used an illegal coagulant called Monsel Solution on Muhammad's cut, which according to Conteh irritated his eyes. Had the cut continued to bleed, Conteh would have won by a technical decision.

An appeal was filed on behalf of Conteh to the WBC and the New Jersey State Commission to change the decision because Ritacco had been previously warned not to use Monsel. A hearing was held in the state commission's office with Jersey Joe presiding. The expert witness, a doctor, went around and round with Ritacco concerning the legality of the coagulant and whether he had broken any rules. The doctor said in his opinion the substance was illegal and Ritacco should receive consequences for his actions. Joe suggested a rematch if Muhammad wanted to retain the title because they knew Ritacco violated the rule. Jersey Joe notified the WBC of his decision and they took it under advisement.

The WBC concluded there should be a rematch between Muhammad and Conteh within 180 days. This would give the fighters ample time to recuperate and train for the upcoming bout. They conducted a purse bid to determine the amount each fighter would earn. Ordinarily, in a purse bid, the winning promoter of a purse bid must give the champion 75% of the total bid and the challenger receives 25% of the bid, but due to the actions of Ritacco Muhammad would receive 55% and Conteh 45%.

The rematch occurred at the same location in Atlantic City on March 29, 1980. The fight was sponsored by the WBC and the New Jersey State Commissioners' office and would air once again on ABC's Wide World of Sports. The fight was going as expected until the fourth round. That's when Muhammad unleashed several body punches catching Conteh off guard. He couldn't handle the onslaught of punches that Muhammad threw at him and Muhammad won by a technical knockout and retained the title.

It seems that when Don King, Butch Lewis, and others saw how successful the Muhammad vs Conteh fight was, they felt they could come to Atlantic City and receive support from the casinos and television stations and successfully promote their boxing matches. Another fight that took place in Atlantic City involved Olympian Howard Davis Jr. and Vilomar Fernandez on February 23, 1980. Davis had never received championship status in the professional ranks even though he was an Olympic champion. The place was crowded full of fans eager to see the fight. Davis prevailed in the twelve-round bout without much difficulty winning by a unanimous decision.

Having these matches opened the doors for Atlantic City, New Jersey to host bigger and better professional championship fights. The State Commissioner's office also sponsored a fight at the Playboy Club in McAfee, New Jersey. We were quickly becoming one of the "big kids on the block" and establishing ourselves as the boxing capital of the east coast. This was a major stepping stone to the many successes that I would experience in boxing.

Jersey Joe was one of the finest guys that I ever worked with, he was with me the entire time to make sure everything was done the right way. He wanted to make sure our reputation in the boxing arena remained spotless. Around this time Bob Arum began doing more promoting of boxing in New Jersey under the aegis of Frank Gelb.

CHAPTER 43

Enter the promoting game a man by the name of Harold Smith. No one seemed to know where Smith came from, and I sensed that something was amiss with him. He seemed to have cash oozing out of every pocket, and he enjoyed flashing it around. Smith always walked around with a briefcase full of cash, and he dominated boxing when it came to paying fighters. If Arum or King paid one million, Smith would pay 1.5 million, and he paid in cash. Smith also paid the managers and trainers in cash because he was seeking their loyalty.

Smith would fly in his plane to fights all around the United States to recruit King and Arum's champions, even though they were still under contract. Most fighters didn't care about the legalities of a contract, all they wanted was the money.

Many discussions were surrounding Smith's acquisition of all the cash that he was dropping around town, but no one seemed to know the answer. Rumors swirled around Smith saying he was running a numbers operation, possible ties to the mob, or that he was a big-time drug dealer. Smith was scheduled to host a show called "This Is It" in New York's Madison Square Garden where he had seven of the world's champions fighting for world title bouts. This infuriated King and Arum because they were both shut out of the event. They threatened Smith with several lawsuits, they knew these events would be momentous.

A few months before the event was scheduled to take place, word came down that Harold Smith was connected to an embezzling scheme at Wells Fargo Bank where nearly 21 million dollars was taken. Smith had someone on the inside of the bank assisting him with the theft. The "you know what" hit the fan" when this information was revealed. The men who thought they were going to get money from Smith now found themselves broke because Smith was broke. The federal government brought charges against Smith and he was sent away to serve a ten-year prison sentence.

CHAPTER 44

For a moment in history, fighters got their money before their managers and promoters. Before Smith, and since he left the scene, managers would receive the money and then give the fighters what they wanted them to have. Harold Smith made it so the fighters would get their prize money and leave out their promoters and managers. As they say, "Turnabout is fair play." At the end of the scandal, the fighters had to eat crow and return to King, Arum, and the other promoters for their representation.

There were several upcoming promoters such as Butch Lewis and Dan Duva with Main Events Promotions who were making a name for themselves. Although this may be disputed, I believe Don King and Bob Arum, especially King, have been good for the business of boxing. I believe many people were intimidated by King's power and total disregard of what people thought about him. Specifically, Caucasians. Arum and King were great to work with because they had better organizations, better matchmaking abilities, and they understood the rules better than most.

When King and Arum said they were going to put on a fight, it was guaranteed to proceed professionally, and they both had strong financial backing. They made sure their fighters got paid. If they hit an economic roadblock, they had the support to continue business as usual. The other promoters couldn't take a financial hit and rebound the way Arum and King could.

Arum and King offered opportunities for the fighters to move from one promoter to another. Arum had most of the middleweight boxers under contract. Promoters and managers had to go through him for those boxers. Don King had most of the heavyweight boxers under contract. If a fighter had a problem with King, he would go to Arum and he would make things better. If a fighter had a problem with Arum, they would go to King, and he would attempt to resolve the fighters' issues. This is how they marketed their agencies. The two promoters were adversaries, but they knew how to conduct business so that each of them could operate successfully. King and Arum were an asset to the fighters even though they were demonized in the press. These promoters were instrumental in creating millionaires out of fighters who never would have seen that kind of money.

As a rule, Arum and King did not work together, but there was one fight in which the duo collaborated on. The fight was known as a BADK Production (Bob Arum Don King) and it was a battle between Sugar Ray Leonard, the champion and Roberto Duran, the challenger. The fight was held in Montreal, Canada on June 20, 1980. They were fighting for the WBC championship. I was invited to keep score ringside for the fight. The bout was scheduled to be aired on Pay Per View on closed-circuit television. The Leonard vs. Duran match was a good fight. People from all over the world watched the match because everyone remembered Sugar Ray as being the 1976 Olympic boxing champion. Duran was the lightweight champion. He moved up in weight so he could fight Leonard for the Welterweight title.

CHAPTER 45

There was a lot of trash-talking between Leonard and Duran before the match. I had been a Sugar Ray fan since I witnessed his skills at the '76 Olympics. Duran was known as "the hands of stone" by his fans and the people's champion. During the fight, it appeared that the two of them were trying to hurt each other. Although it was a close fight, Duran won the bout by a unanimous decision. I thought the fight was very close, but I wasn't a judge. The judges called the fight the way they saw it. When Duran won the title, the promotional rights went to Don King, so he called for a rematch.

The Duran vs Leonard rematch was scheduled for November 26, 1980, at the Louisiana Superdome in New Orleans. At the time of the match, I was working with the WBA as a North American representative for championships and I attended the executive meeting in Puerto Rico. Bob Arum was in attendance, but he wasn't associated with the production. King was in charge. After our banquet, they set up a large screen for us to watch the fight. Everyone had an opinion on how they thought the fight would turn out, but opinions are like noses...everybody has one.

From the start of the rematch Leonard was moving swiftly, this made it difficult for Duran to keep up with him. Sometime around the eighth round, Duran turned his back to Sugar Ray and uttered the now-famous words "No mas," He quit! Leonard walked over to Duran and hit him again. Duran walked away which frustrated Leonard to no end, but he was happy to have regained his title. I stood up and shouted at the screen. I couldn't believe what happened. The commentator, Howard Cossell, yelled, "Duran said no mas, no mas. He quit!" Bob Arum was stunned by the turn of events in the ring. We celebrated and hugged each other because we were both Leonard fans. I was happy that Sugar Ray Leonard was again the Welterweight champion. Duran was never the same after that match.

King and Arum worked together when it was in their best interest for business or financially. It was common knowledge that there was no love lost between Arum and King, and the fighters benefitted from their adversarial relationship. The two of them gave many fighters a chance to fight professionally and make money while doing it. There were new promoters who began to creep up the ladder of success by gaining top-ranked fighters.

CHAPTER 46

The driving force behind boxing is keeping the promoters at the forefront of the sport. Therefore, Don King was successful as a promoter. He always had champions that he could put in the ring who were able to defeat their opponents. This made King unpopular, he could out-hustle the other promoters and they would be angry with his success. King didn't sit around waiting for boxers to find him. He went out and recruited talented fighters. Eventually, King was known worldwide, not only for his talent as a promoter but also for his unique hairstyle. Whenever King was photographed there was never any confusion as to who he was. Many promoters had to crawl and scratch their way up in boxing, but none reached the level of success of Don King and Bob Arum.

ROUND 12
SOUTHPAW

CHAPTER 47

It wasn't two weeks later that Bob Arum, the president of Top Rank Boxing congratulated me on our new organization. He said the IBF ratings suggested Marvin Hagler was our middleweight champion. I told him that he was correct. Arum was Marvelous Marvin Hagler's promoter and he said Hagler wanted to defend his title against Wilford Scypion. Hagler was the middleweight champion of the WBA and WBC. The fight was scheduled to take place a few weeks after the inception of the IBF.

I received a call from Arum saying he was sorry for the way things turned out in Puerto Rico. He suggested that there was a chance for me to get even with the other federations by sponsoring the upcoming Hagler-Scypion match. Arum said Hagler was planning to defend his title on May 27, 1983, in Providence, Rhode Island. He wanted to go fifteen rounds, which was against the WBA and WBC rules, and he was threatening to walk away from the fight if his demand for fifteen rounds were not met. Hagler felt he had won the title in fifteen rounds, so he wanted this match to be the same. Arum said Hagler needed my support.

I agreed to sponsor the match recognizing it as the perfect opportunity to legitimize the IBF. I was tickled to death to be a part of this momentous event. I appointed some officials for the fight, and we took the train to Rhode Island. One of IBF's executive committee members and legal counsel, Walter Stone, was also the commissioner in Providence. The people of Rhode Island were very hospitable, and Hagler was excited that the IBF approved the fifteen-round fight.

After my arrival in Providence, Stone and I assigned the officials, attended the rules meeting, and conducted the weigh-in. We got everything squared away. The press was hyping up the fight saying the IBF broke the mold set by the other federations by allowing the fight to go fifteen rounds. The fight began and both Hagler and Scypion were holding their own, but by the fifth round, Hagler began to demolish his opponent. Hagler knocked out Scypion in the fourth round. Marvelous Marvin Hagler became IBF's first official champion.

CHAPTER 48

Returning home from Rhode Island on the train, there were some reporters onboard from the New York area. They surrounded me and began throwing dozens of questions my way. They were asking about the fifteen round bouts, South Africa boxers, and why we started the IBF. I answered the questions as best I could. I was glad when we finally made it to New York so that I could escape the barrage of questions. I knew that I had to find a way to formally introduce the IBF to the world.

The media took shots at the IBF calling us alphabet soup. They couldn't imagine another boxing organization, especially one with an African American at the helm. They refused to give the IBF any support. I called a press conference to alert the promoters that the IBF was here to stay. I decided to have a press conference in the media capital of the world, New York City. My public relations manager, Sy Roseman, knew that I was having a difficult time finding a location to hold the press conference. Sy suggested I contact a young African American man named Gil Chapman who had just been appointed public relations manager for the Giants Stadium in East Rutherford. I decided to give it a shot and contact Mr. Chapman, a man who had been a tremendous football player at Thomas Jefferson High School in Elizabeth, New Jersey.

I called Gil Chapman and told him that I was a fan of his from his football days in high school. I told him that I was looking for a location to hold a press conference for the newly formed International Boxing Federation. Chapman asked if I would like to hold the press conference at the stadium. I was ecstatic and accepted the offer. I asked if the press conference could be held within the next two weeks. Gil said two weeks would give him enough time to plan an event like no one had ever seen before. It would be the talk of the town. He said that not only would the boxing media be invited, but he would reach out to the football press. Chapman said he would do whatever was needed. All I had to do was show up at 1 pm on the day of the event. I was grateful to Sy for making the connection between Chapman and me.

Notices were sent out to inform the public of the press conference announcing the formation of the IBF at the Giant's stadium. I was pleased with the beauty of the location. The press was set up in an area surrounded by glass allowing an amazing view of the field. I was pleased that Chapman included this area for the press conference. There was plenty of food. Everything from soup to steak, it was set up buffet style.

The press who covered boxing came from the New York Times, The Daily News, and The Post. Television reporters were walking around eating and taking in the beauty of the press area. I introduced Sy to Gil Chapman, and Gil asked us if the event met our expectations. We watched the writers gorging themselves on food and experiencing the classy accommodations for the first time. We told Gil, this event was sure to etch the acronym IBF in the minds of the boxing media for years to come.

CHAPTER 49

After the meal, I took to the podium and thanked everyone for coming. I extended an invitation to the reporters to convene in a nearby conference room where they could continue enjoying the atmosphere and the buffet. We knew they would be curious about the business that was about to take place, so I instructed Gil to turn on the intercom in the room that housed the reporters for them to hear the meeting. It wasn't that I cared about them knowing what was going on with the IBF, I sent them to another room to avoid unnecessary interruptions.

Don King and Marty Cohen from Florida were two of the promoters in attendance. They came to lambaste me for approving South African boxers to be added to the ratings. King stood up in the meeting to ask how could I as a Black man have business dealings with people from South Africa when I was aware of how they were treating people of color. Cohen chimed in with the same rhetoric. I was so infuriated by what they were saying that I had to compose myself before responding. I told them they could say what they wanted, but I was a part of the Civil Rights Movement, donating my money and my time. I expressed to them how I pounded the pavement to help my people gain equality, and I was aware of how people of color were hurting, these boxers were hurting. All they wanted was a chance. As far as I was concerned if they didn't fight in South Africa, I didn't feel that I was doing anything wrong.

Everyone knew that things would change once Nelson Mandela took over, but until then we had to make do with what we had. Of course, the only person who continued to protest was Don King, everyone else was okay with the South African boxers. Lou Duva commented that I was just trying to give the young boxers a break. Someone else remarked that I was just trying to open doors for those who had had doors closed in their faces.

Lou Duva was known to be boisterous. When he talked everybody listened. He and Don King got into a shouting match, which was a continuation of the drama from the WBA convention. Lou Duva told King that he didn't care what he did. He told him to go back over there with the WBC and watch your guys disintegrate. We are going to make the IBF the greatest organization of all time. The New Jersey News along with the New York Daily News and the New York Post gave a thumbs up to the launch of the IBF. They began conducting on the spot interviews. They invited me to come to their newsroom on Broad Street in Newark, New Jersey, since it was so close to the stadium, for a segment on their news that evening. They wanted me to share with their viewers the IBF's plans.

As the event came to an end my legal counsel Walter Stone and Alvin Goodwin said if I had any legal questions before the interview, they were ready to assist. I told them I was sure that I could handle the reporter on my own. As I prepared to leave the stadium Bill Brennan offered to go with me to the studio.

Brennan and I were miked for the show and prepared to be interviewed. The reporter was supportive and for an hour asked numerous questions about the formation of the IBF. I did most of the talking since Brennan hadn't been with the organization that long. We both thought the interview went well.

As we walked back to our cars, we were confronted by none other than Don King. King insisted that he didn't know why I was the head of a federation when I didn't know what I was doing. He said he didn't know how far I was going with the organization, but from his experience, the Latinos were going to stick together and leave me out in the cold. I told King that wouldn't happen if I had the support of people in America. King insisted that I was going to have Black folks up in arms against me. I told him I would have to accept their anger because I felt like I was doing the right thing for my people. Before I started working with the State Athletic Commission there were no Black officials in this area. There were only two Black officials and they were from Las Vegas.

Joe and I made a difference for our people in boxing. I had to remind Don that he didn't have an all-Black staff working for him, so I told him he was being a hypocrite and I didn't appreciate him kicking me in the teeth in front of all those people. You need the black and white keys on the piano to make good music and I intended to pull everybody together. Don King and I shook hands and agreed to disagree, but I felt that in the end, we would make history in the sport of boxing. I made the decision that I was going to create change with this new federation and if I had to lose a few people along the way, that was the sacrifice I was willing to make.

CHAPTER 50

Sy was an asset to the IBF because he knew how to get things done. He was one of those guys who could boast that he could sell sand on the beach. People had a hard time telling him no. Following the convention, the IBF held an executive committee meeting in Reno, Nevada. Many commissioners from around the world were invited to join the IBF. The event was being held at the El Dorado Hotel in Reno. Officials came from the Philippines, Korea, and a few from Japan, all willing to help the IBF because they had been shut out by the WBA and WBC. They saw this as an opportunity to open the doors and gain champions for their country. We appointed an official from Japan to be the vice president. A gentleman from Korea who was an interpreter could handle our South Korea business. North Korea was not interested in being a part of the IBF. A few fights were set up in the Philippines and South Korea. They encouraged me to come to extend my blessings on the match. I didn't attend but I sent our International Commissioner, Jim Stevenson, who was a gentlemen's gentleman and was great at making sure things went smoothly.

The IBF added a couple of Korean and Philippian champions to our rankings and added matches in Tokyo, Japan. The Japanese commission wouldn't interfere with the boxing matches, but we knew we wouldn't get any action in Tokyo. People worldwide supported the IBF because we opened doors that had once been closed. We made it possible for countries to have champions that never had them before.

Right after the press conference in the Giant's Stadium in East Rutherford, New Jersey, word began to circulate about the IBF. We were approached by a thirty-one-year-old American Indian boxer by the name of Marvin Camel from Montana. He wanted to compete for the vacant Cruiserweight title. We gave him permission and the fight took place on

December 13, 1983, against Roddy MacDonald in Nova Scotia, Canada. Camel won the title by a TKO in round five of fifteen rounds. He was so proud of his win that he would walk around town showing off his championship belt. He then defended the title again in Billings, Montana against Lee Roy Murphy. I sent Bill Brennan as a representative for the IBF because I was unable to attend. Camel lost the match with a controversial TKO in the 14th round due to a seemingly serious gash above his left eye. Camel didn't want the fight to be called off, but Dan Jancic the referee ended the fight toward the end of the fourteenth round. Murphy was escorted from the ring through a crowd that booed his victory. Camel remained in the ring and received cheers from his fans.

CHAPTER 51

It was time for the IBF's official coming-out bash. The founding convention was to be held in November of 1983 in Newark, New Jersey at the Quality Inn Hotel. That's when we changed the name from the USBA-I to the USBA-IBF. Originally, we wanted to host the convention in the Catskills of New York. We realized it would be too difficult for people to get there, so we decided upon a more accessible location. Although the office in the Quality Inn was up and running, it wasn't as nice as I would have liked it to be, but it was starting to shape up. We couldn't afford much more because the money for the organization was coming from Brennan and my pockets. We weren't discouraged because we had a dream and we were determined to make it happen. We knew sacrifices would have to be made.

Carolyn Kelly Shabazz one of boxing's first female promoters and gym owner oversaw the entertainment for the convention. She also included a furrier who displayed a variety of fur coats and jackets for men and women. After a request from Stan Hoffman, a record producer for Savoy Records, we hired a singer named Evelyn Champagne King. We also invited comedian and activist Dick Gregory. He had the people rolling in the aisles. We didn't have as many people in attendance as we thought we would have, so we took a bath on the event. We did have a nice showing from people who came from other states. Arum arranged for a bus to take our guests to the Resort Casino in Atlantic City, and they returned around two in the morning after a night of partying and gambling. People had time to recuperate because we didn't start our business until nine in the morning. Carolyn and I expected a larger turnout, but we did the best we could, even though we were coming up a little short on some of our financial obligations from the convention. Butch Lewis was a big help by offering me cash to pay the hotel bill. Brennan and I were both using our American Express cards to cover the remaining expenses. We were struggling but we were still holding on. I refused to let the powers that be outhustle me. I planned to be successful and to take those with me who wanted to come.

We started to be noticed by officials from other countries. We began going to Italy, England, and Australia. We were already in the Far East. I gave many fighters a chance that wouldn't have otherwise made it in boxing, but as soon as they would get the wrinkles out of their bellies, they would run right back to the White man. Many of them often forgot about the bridge that brought them across to success.

CHAPTER 52

Some guys came from Korea, Philippines, and Japan requested several fights they wanted to sponsor with boxers who were rated. Our sponsorship would give credence to their request. We had many countries in the world supporting us, however, the Japanese rejected us. When I ran for the WBA presidency and lost, they put a Japanese man in as vice president, and he didn't want to recognize the IBF. He wanted to eliminate our organization. We were a target, they were trying to get rid of us, but I never let that get to me. I was bound and determined to succeed, and I wasn't giving up on my dreams. One guy seemed surprised that I was still around. I told him that my head may be bloodied, but it was still unbowed. I knew they weren't going to do anything to me because I had the protection of the good Lord.

The IBF started to climb up the ladder and I was making numerous public appearances to help the promoters in the Far East, Korea, and Japan. There were promoters in Japan, but they didn't have the blessings of the Japanese boxing commissioner. They had outlaw promotions going on in Osaka, Japan. The people there welcomed us with open arms, they were excited and supportive of the IBF organization. They seemed to like seeing an American organization with a Black man at the helm. We had some memorable fights in Korea and the Philippines. One year my wife went with me and we almost got run out of town due to the decision of one of the fights. Cooler heads prevailed and we managed to make it out safely.

We had some good fighters emerge from the far east including a boxer from Seoul, South Korea named Chong Pal Park. Park weighed 168 pounds which was big for a Korean. He fought like a tiger, and he fought six or seven times in defense of his title. He was listed as one of the best in the world. He eventually left the IBF and his career was never the same. I saw it as poetic justice.

ROUND 13

POUND FOR POUND

CHAPTER 53

We had to make some changes in the IBF executive committee because Francis Walker, who was the ratings chairman, had to work under Binns, who opposed me when I ran for the WBA. He decided to torment Walker and make his life a living hell. Walker decided to resign. That's when we brought in Doug Beavers. More on him later. During this time, I was president of the USBA-IBF, the deputy commissioner, and acting commissioner in the state of New Jersey. The word was the attorney general said: "That is too much power for one man to have." A statement that was also uttered about the late Malcolm X. Translated that meant too much power for one Black man to have.

On the state level, the attorney general started to chip away at me. Little by little he and some of his friends tried to undermine me and my work with the IBF. The attorney general's weapon of choice was to bring phony charges against me for ethics violations. When I opened the office in Newark, we didn't have any equipment. One of our referees, Joe Cortez, was helping to clean up and haul the contents from some of the buildings. When we found out that he was cleaning some of the buildings, we asked him if we could buy some of the surplus furniture. Joe said that because he was a member of the organization, he would donate the furniture to the IBF. Cortez donated some desks, file cabinets, and chairs.

One day Frank Gelb said he needed a copy of something, and I told him he would have to wait until I went to the place on Route 22 that copies things for me. I told him that we didn't have a copy machine. Frank said he would see what he could do about getting one for our office. Gelb contacted Arum and suggested that he donate a copy machine. Arum said he would gladly contribute a copy machine to our office. Another member volunteered to donate some carpet to help spruce up the office. Along comes the ethic panel saying that as the president of the IBF and the acting commissioner, soliciting favors from people is in direct violation of the ethics rules. I asked for a hearing on the matter because I knew that I had done nothing wrong. I employed two Black attorneys to represent me, and I had a string of witnesses ready to testify. The day before the hearing they called to tell me that the hearing had been postponed. I asked why, and they said the hearing officer and ethics committee called it off. My attorneys said they would do some research and get in contact with me once they had more information.

I informed my witnesses that the hearing had been canceled, so they didn't need to show up. Three months later I received a notification telling me that the administrative office held a hearing and determined that I violated the ethics rules by soliciting at least six people that I had regulatory control over. I asked my attorneys what happened to my notification to attend the hearing. They said they had no idea what had happened. Apparently, some backroom deal had been made, I don't know who did it, if my attorneys did it under my name, or whether I had been taken advantage of. I was suspended for six months. At that moment I knew that I had a target on my back, and they were aiming straight at it. They were coming after me for the deputy commissioners' position because they recognized that the IBF had become a formidable organization. The attorney general didn't want me having two high profile positions. When I left on suspension, I took all my belongings because I knew I would not return. When I contacted some of the guys on the executive committee to inform them that I had been placed on suspension, I told them that I would work full time for the IBF. They all agreed to my offer. They wanted to know if there were enough funds to pay me. I told them that Weitzel said there were enough funds in the treasury to pay me a salary equal to what I was receiving from the government. I dropped the commissionership and went into the IBF full time.

CHAPTER 54

The boxing match that put the IBF on the map both in America and internationally was October of 1983 when Larry Holmes was the heavyweight champion of the WBC. Holmes and WBC president Sulamin got into a public shouting match with Holmes cussing in English and Sulamin in Spanish. They almost came to blows. After the confrontation, Larry declared that he would never fight for the WBC again. This left Holmes an ex-champion without a title. The incident was highlighted in the sports section of the newspaper worldwide.

Murad Muhammad, the first Black promoter in New Jersey, promoted matches in several cities, including Atlantic City and Las Vegas. He was a successful promoter who I gave his first promoting license in 1976 when I was the deputy commissioner. Muhammad called me with a dilemma. He said Larry Holmes had just walked out on the WBC after getting into a cussing match, which included him and Sulamin talking about each other's mamas. Muhammad explained that Holmes had nowhere to fight even though he had a 45-0 record. Murad said that Holmes was going after Marciano's 49-0 record as a heavyweight champion, but without a title, he wouldn't be able to fight for a championship. Muhammad suggested that I allow Holmes to fight under the IBF organization so that he could continue his pursuit of Marciano's record. I asked him for some time to think about his request.

I later told Muhammad that because Larry Holmes was African American, I felt obligated to help him. I instructed Murad to arrange a meeting with Holmes, Jersey Joe, and Cora Wilds, the chairman of the D.C. boxing commission. Also in attendance were Walter Stone, an attorney for the IBF, Carolyn Shabazz, boxing promoter and member of the IBF, and a few other officials to hear Holmes plead his case. Two days later Muhammad brought Holmes to the IBF office at the Quality Inn, where an elaborate spread had been set up by the hotel's manager to impress Larry Holmes. After enjoying the refreshments, we got down to the business at hand.

Muhammad opened the discussion revealing that Holmes was no longer the WBC heavyweight champion and the WBA title was held by Gerrie Coetzee. The IBF was the only organization without a heavyweight champion. Holmes began to plead his case. I couldn't stand hearing him grovel anymore as Holmes stood before the group with tears in his eyes. I told Holmes to stand up and be a man. I explained that he was the heavyweight champion of the world, so I expected him to address the group as such. Jersey Joe explained to Larry that he too had been a proud heavyweight champion, and it was a great position to be in. Jersey Joe continued telling him that there was no reason to exhibit that type of bow and scrape behavior toward the committee. He told Holmes that he would have had more respect for him if he had come in arguing for the right to be champion as opposed to begging the committee for an opportunity. Jersey Joe told Larry that as the IBF's heavyweight champion he would have to conduct himself like a champion. Several members of the committee shouted out that they agreed with Joe. Larry apologized to the group, stating that he had admired Jersey Joe as a boxer ever since he was a kid. He said that he appreciated the opportunity to present his case.

Several of Holmes's friends were in attendance, including the head of the NAACP of Eastern Pennsylvania. He applauded the IBF saying he was glad for the organization because it showed what we could do as a people if we stuck together. He said that he appreciated the IBF allowing Holmes to regain his title which enabled him to go after Marciano's record.

I adjourned the meeting to give the committee time to decide. I addressed the committee telling them that this was our opportunity to do something for someone who was a minority and needed help. I told them that if we didn't give Holmes a chance that someone else might. If he conducted himself like a champion and followed the rules and regulations of the International Boxing Federation, I told them that I was all for bringing Holmes on board. Jersey Joe agreed that Larry should be the IBF's heavyweight champion, and we should support his pursuit of Marciano's record. The rest of the committee agreed. This was especially important to

Jersey Joe because Marciano whooped him twice. We called Holmes back into the room and told him it would be an honor to have him represent the IBF as our heavyweight champion. Holmes promised to be a role model for our organization and said he appreciated the opportunity. I was pleased that we had a show of solidarity among brothers. News spread quickly that Larry Holmes had been brought on as IBF's heavyweight champion. The headline in many newspaper sports sections across the country stated that the IBF corralled Larry Holmes as their heavyweight champion.

CHAPTER 55

arry Holmes' first fight was scheduled to be held in Las Vegas, Nevada at
the Riviera Hotel and Casino November 9, 1984, against Bone Crusher
Smith. The manager of the hotel expressed his gratitude to the IBF for
bringing the fight to their location. He was also excited by the crowds of
people who had gathered in the lobby of the hotel waiting to get Holmes'
autograph. It was ironic because this was the same manager who threatened
to throw me out of the hotel if I didn't pay a 14,000-dollar hotel bill that
didn't belong to me. Larry went on to defeat Bone Crusher Smith by a
TKO in the twelfth round of the fifteen-round match.

Holmes' next fight was against David Bey on March 15, 1985. Holmes
won by a TKO in round ten of a fifteen round bout. He then fought Carl
"The Truth" Williams May 20, 1985, a controversial fight that many still
question how Larry Holmes won the decision. We were getting excited
because Holmes was closing in on Marciano's record. Larry stayed true
to his word and represented the IBF in an upstanding manner. He gave
credit to our organization and said he was proud to be our heavyweight
champion. Holmes became the IBF's standard-bearer. That's when trouble
started brewing.

The IBF usually held executive meetings twice a year. Around
1985 when we were preparing for our meeting, Luis Tabuena a member
appointed to our growing executive committee and high ranking official in
the Philippines games and amusement board notified us that the president
of the Philippine Ferdinand Marcos invited us to hold our meeting at
Manilla. The expenses would be handled by the Philippine country.

The members of the executive committee in the United States gathered
in San Francisco, California and from there we all flew to Manila. Mr.
Tabuena who was the overseer of activities at the airport in Manilla

arranged to meet us at the airport. We were chauffeured to an exclusive hotel, the location of our lodging and meetings.

Once we settled in and had lunch, Mr. Tabuena had cars waiting to take us to President Marcos' office. When we arrived, welcomed with open arms and President Marcos and I talked like we were old friends. His office was adorned with photos, awards, and plaques from around the world that had been presented to him by fellow dignitaries. He shared the history of the ones that he was especially proud of.

President Marcos thanked me for establishing the IBF which allowed Filipino boxer, Dodie Boy Penalosa to become a world champion. He said the other organizations had sidestepped their duties by not allowing Philippine fighters to excel in boxing. When the IBF came along, we gave hope and support to the fighters of Marcos' country.

Mrs. Imelda Marcos, the first lady of the Phillippines, entered the room. As customary on my part, I stood and acknowledged the presence of this charming lady. She participated in an engaging conversation with Mr. Tabuena, President Marcos, and me. Finally, the president asked his wife if she would be available that evening to take us to dinner. She said that she was, and Mr. Tabuena told her that we would be ready at 6:00 pm. Mrs. Marcos took us to an elegant restaurant where we would enjoy the evening festivities.

We were escorted into a private room. Sixteen of us sat around a horseshoe-shaped table. Mr. Tabuena insisted that I sit next to Imelda Marcos on one side and a friend who accompanied her sat on the other side. We each had our own waiter at our beck and call. They brought our meal on a silver domed platter. In unison, they all lifted the lids to expose the delicacy that was hidden beneath.

As we prepared for dessert after our meal, our fourth vice president Alvin Goodman, a talented magician, stood in the middle of the horseshoe and performed some magic tricks. The crowd was delighted. After an evening of good conversation and a few magic tricks, we returned to our rooms to prepare for the meetings to be held the next day.

CHAPTER 56

Michael Spinks, the IBF's light heavyweight champion wanted to fight Larry Holmes for the heavyweight title because that's where the money was. Butch Lewis was Spinks manager and promoter. Murad Muhammad promoted Holmes' first two fights, then Holmes jumped ship and went with Don King because he knew he would make more money. Loyalty was not a strong suit for many fighters. Spinks began targeting Holmes with a war of words after one of his matches. He described how he would whoop Holmes and challenged him to a fight. The press ate up the public rants and encouraged Spinks behavior, and wrote headlines touting a Holmes-Spinks battle. Jersey Joe and I both told Holmes not to fight Spinks because Marciano's record was within reach. We encouraged him to box fighters who were further down on the ratings list. Holmes declared that he was going to teach Spinks a lesson by defeating him in the ring. It didn't help that Butch Lewis was baiting Holmes into a match with Spinks. He told Larry when Spinks finished beating up on him, he was going to whoop him too. I tried to persuade Holmes to stay away from Michael Spinks because he was a smarter fighter than Holmes. Spinks was tall and lean, but very strong. Larry continued saying that he was going to fight and win against Spinks. I thought it was the lure of the purse that convinced Holmes to risk breaking Marciano's record. Don King was pushing the fight from one side and Butch Lewis was pushing from the other side. Joe and I tried in vain to stall the inevitable, but they ended up scheduling the fight for September 21, 1985, at the Riviera Hotel and Casino in Las Vegas.

Spinks defeated Holmes by a unanimous decision after the fifteen-round bout. This was the first time a light heavyweight contender defeated a heavyweight champion. Throughout the fight, Spinks outmaneuvered Holmes. Every time Holmes would try to throw a punch, Spinks would beat him to it. Spinks was on his game that night. Muhammad Ali talked about Holmes like a dog. He said, "Anytime a light heavyweight champion tries to move up on a heavyweight champion, you are supposed to defeat them. You let Spinks whoop you."

CHAPTER 57

After the Spinks-Holmes fight, I retired to my room. Murad Muhammad called me to say, "God don't like ugly. After all that I did for Holmes, he went to work for King and cut me out of the picture." Muhammad said although he wasn't happy to see Holmes lose, he didn't stand a chance in the ring with Spinks. Holmes still had a promotion agreement with Muhammad when he signed with Don King. Muhammad had to threaten Holmes with a lawsuit to collect his money.

The day after the fight when we arrived at the airport, Marian Muhammad, our executive secretary, Al Lucas and I were using the curbside to check-in our luggage. Suddenly, a long white limousine pulled up and out steps Larry Holmes and his entourage. Holmes got in my face and began cussing me saying it was Butch Lewis and my fault that he lost his title. Everyone was shocked as they watched Holmes rant and rave about losing the fight while standing toe to toe with me. Holmes' wife and bodyguards witnessed his public tirade. Finally, a Caucasian man who was standing nearby intervened. He stepped to Holmes and asked him what his problem was, He told Larry if he had used the same energy that he was exhibiting at the airport last night, he wouldn't have lost the fight. The man told Holmes he got in the ring and didn't half fight but wanted to come out here and fight this guy because you couldn't retain your title. The man told Larry that he should be ashamed of himself. It was a shame that it took a White man to calm him down. Mariam said she thought Holmes was going to hit me. I told her I thought the same thing, and I hoped he wasn't going to be on the same plane as us because I'm not a fighter. My only defense would have been to pick up a stick or something and hit him with it. Fortunately, they were on a different flight.

CHAPTER 58

Larry Holmes owed the IBF over 50,000 dollars in sanctioning fees and refused to pay. When I called him to inquire about his debt, his secretary said that Larry didn't wish to speak to me. I expressed to her that I didn't want to speak to him either, I only wanted him to pay what he owed. The secretary said that Mr. Holmes was not going to pay the fees. I paid a visit to the ratings chairman to have him drop Holmes from the ratings. Once the IBF and WBC dropped Holmes from the ratings, and if he couldn't fight anyone in the WBA, he was at a loss for a title. Holmes still refused to pay. I never harassed him about the money because I knew that eventually, he would want a rematch with Spinks. When Murad Muhammad contacted me saying that Holmes was trying to get a rematch with Spinks, I told Muhammad that it wasn't possible because Larry wasn't in the ratings and he still owed sanctioning fees. I informed Murad that the television stations wouldn't sponsor a Holmes fight because he was no longer the heavyweight champion. Murad said that he could possibly persuade Holmes to pay the past due fees. I explained that not only would Larry have to pay the past due fees, he would also have to pay the sanction fees for the upcoming fight. If he paid the entire amount the IBF would consider adding him to the ratings and approve the fight, if the Championship Chairman agreed.

Holmes sent me the checks as required. Murad asked if I had received the money. I told him that I had but I was waiting to make sure the checks cleared. The IBF reinstated Holmes into the ratings and told HBO that Holmes and Spinks would have a rematch for the heavyweight title. The purse for this fight would be substantial for both fighters. Holmes would receive 1.5 million dollars compared to Spinks 3.5 million dollars. HBO was in the process of producing a series searching for the one and only heavyweight champion. This fight, scheduled for April 1986 in Las Vegas, was scheduled to be a part of the HBO series.

Holmes and Spinks battled it out in a rematch. Spinks once again defeated Holmes with a fifteen round split decision. Holmes was an 8-5 favorite, but experts said Holmes was no match for Spink's left hook. Holmes was angry. He claimed that he had won the fight. He said the judges had " lying eyes". I had to admit that it was a very close fight, but Holmes didn't perform well enough to take the championship from Spinks.

The next fight was the battle between Michael Spinks and Mike Tyson to determine who would be the next Heavyweight champ. Both men were undefeated. The fight was scheduled for June 27, 1988, in Atlantic City. It was a memorable fight because less than two minutes into the bout, Tyson knocked Spinks out. Tyson became the WBA, WBC, the IBF heavyweight champion, and he won the HBO series. This made Tyson the Universal Heavyweight champion.

Mike Tyson and Bobby Lee

CHAPTER 59

D on King, Tyson's promoter, encouraged Tyson to head to Japan to fight Buster Douglas at the Tokyo Dome on February 11, 1990. Tyson was favored 42-1. The fight was dubbed "Tyson is Back!" The Japanese Boxing commission snubbed the IBF who was scheduled to receive the sanction fees that Tyson and Douglas would generate. The Japanese commission didn't like that our federation was involved in this monumental fight.

I decided not to go to Tokyo to the Tyson-Douglas fight because I had just taken a long flight less than two weeks before to Nagoya, Japan. Thirteen-hour flights can do a number on you, and I didn't want to go again so soon. I called Don King to inform him that I wouldn't be attending, but the IBF supported his champion, Mike Tyson. King said that he and Tyson were both ready to leave Tokyo because he was tired of eating the food in Tokyo. Don said that all Tyson wanted to do was get into the ring, knock Buster out, and get on the plane so he could get a good homecooked meal. I told King to wish Tyson luck and I would be in touch with them when they returned.

My wife and I were preparing to go to church when I got a call from cornerman and boxing commentator Ferdie Pacheco aka The Fight Doctor, asking what I planned to do about Tyson. I asked him what I was supposed to do with Tyson. Pacheco asked if I knew that had Tyson lost the fight the previous night. I couldn't believe my ears. Everyone thought Tyson was going to defeat Douglas. Ferdie said no one would even bet on the fight because Tyson was the superior fighter. I explained that I didn't see the match on HBO the previous evening. Pacheco said that Douglas knocked Tyson out in the tenth round, and they are calling it the greatest upset in sports history. Ferdie told me Jose Sulamin of WBC and Mendoza of the WBA are both in Japan. I was the only one available to deal with the chaos.

ROUND 14

PRIZE FIGHTER

CHAPTER 60

I knew something was up when the next call I received was from Don King. He explained how the Japanese commission ruled the Tyson-Douglas fight no-contest because the referee didn't adhere to the count properly. King told me not to go along with the decision because Tyson got knocked out fair and square. According to King, they were attempting to steal the title from Douglas and give it back to Mike Tyson. I told Don that I was going to send for the footage and give my assessment of the fight. I told Don I would handle it as soon as I left church.

I had a friend who recorded all the fights, so I asked him to bring the recording to my house. When I viewed the footage, I knew without a doubt Buster Douglas had won the fight. Tyson was clearly dazed, unable to locate his mouthpiece, which was hanging from his mouth. Tyson had no idea where he was. Buster kept his left fist in Tyson's face all night. Tyson became frustrated. He was used to entering the ring and knocking his opponents around. Douglas made a promise to his mother before she died that he was going to defeat Mike Tyson. The crowd went wild because they were able to witness the great Mike Tyson get beat.

Don King approached Sulamin on the plane ride home disagreeing with the no-contest decision. King asked for a rematch to take place within 120 days. Sulamin was open to the suggestion and said he was sure Mendoza would support the rematch. Buster Douglas' people reached out asking me to stop this injustice from taking place. His manager, John Johnson of Ohio, pleaded with me to sort this out. I told him to give me a few days to handle the situation, but in the meantime tell Buster to enjoy his victory. I continued to receive calls asking me what I planned to do about the decision. The question many of them had was, would I follow Sulamin and Mendoza and give the title to Tyson, or would I return it to Douglas. I told them the winner of the fight is the person who is standing after the final count.

Bill Maher from Channel 5 News asked to conduct a live interview at the station. He offered to send a car to pick me up. I put on my suit and waited for the car. I arrived around 10:30 pm to prepare for the 11 o'clock news. Bill's interview focused on the Tyson-Douglas fight, and I reminded him that Douglas was the one standing at the end of the fight so that says it all. No matter what anybody says, Buster Douglas is the heavyweight champion. I told Maher that Tyson lost his title in the ring, no one outside the ring had to take it from him. Bill was glad that I was going to be fair and make the right decision. I offered Maher the opportunity to have Douglas come by the station and receive his accolades from his fans.

CHAPTER 61

The next day NBC contacted me to interview at their station with Len Berman. I told them that I had a previous engagement at Madison Square Garden, but I would come by once I left there. My meeting was with Bobby Goodman, a matchmaker who tried to act like he had something to do with the Tyson-Douglas decision. I was surprised when Berman showed up at the Madison Square Garden to invite me to be a part of the upcoming five o'clock news segment. I told Berman that I would agree to the interview on one condition, and that was he had to introduce me to the very attractive Sue Simmons, a newscaster whom I followed on NBC. I only wanted to shake her hand and say hello. Goodman and I arrived at NBC and was pleased when Berman called me over to introduce me to Simmons. Berman and I went on to discuss the controversy surrounding the Tyson-Douglas fight. Berman said people were amazed about my stance on the dispute. I told him that I was doing what was right. It didn't make sense how some people were determined to take the title from Douglas. The station allowed calls from viewers during the interview. Many callers congratulated me on making the right decision. Don King threatened a lawsuit against the IBF because he felt Tyson deserved the win. I reminded King that I too had a team of attorneys prepared to challenge his suit and file a counter-suit.

Buster Douglas came to Newark for the ceremony to receive his championship belt. I reached out to Carolyn Kelly who helped me contact Mayor Sharpe James to ask him about sponsoring a luncheon at the Quality Inn, the location of the IBF's offices, to celebrate Douglas' victory. I arrived at the airport and waited for Douglas and some of his people to land. When Buster and his manager Mr. Johnson deplaned, they were trying to locate me in the crowd. Mayor James and I took everyone into the terminal and lead them to a podium that had been set up for the occasion. I talked to the crowd about how great the fight had been and how excited I was for Douglas. Mr. Johnson stood up and talked about how pleased he was with my sense of fairness in declaring Douglas the heavyweight champ. Finally, it was Buster's turn to address the crowd. He thanked the people of Newark and promised to return soon. Mayor James closed the celebration and we all went to enjoy the meal at the Quality Inn.

Buster Douglas' next scheduled fight against Evander Holyfield was May 30, 1987, at the Las Vegas Hilton. Holyfield defeated Buster Douglas in the tenth round of a fifteen-round match. Douglas only had himself to blame for the defeat. Once he won against Tyson, he was set up in a room complete with all the amenities. This led to his prefight training being done mostly at the buffet table in the hotel. Buster gained a lot of weight and by the time he became serious about his training, it was too late. He basically gave the heavyweight title to Evander Holyfield.

CHAPTER 62

With New Jersey's addition of casinos, it became the ideal location for boxing matches. I was grateful to have Jersey Joe by my side helping to steer me in the right direction. I didn't mind the moments when he would correct any mistakes that I made or any errors in judgment regarding boxing.

I noticed when I attended matches in New Jersey, there were no Black officials. No Black referees or judges. I expressed my concerns to Joe. He suggested we take some of the Black fighters who knew how the judging process worked and hire them for those positions. We hired Milo Savage (his government name was George Ware) of Salt Lake City, Utah. He became our first Black referee. Then we hired our first Black woman judge Frances Moore. She was sent to us by the Amateur Association. Larry Hazzard was our second Black referee who eventually went on to become a commissioner for the state of New Jersey. He succeeded me in the position.

There was a woman from California named Gwen Adair, she looked like a model. She wanted to be a referee in the worst way. The only matches they would allow her to referee in California were matches with smaller men. When she heard that I was the IBF's president she came to one of our conventions and made a sincere pitch to join our team. After speaking to her at length, I contacted the commissioner from California to learn more about Ms. Adair. He said he didn't think Adair had the upper body strength to control some of the fighters. After speaking with the people in California, I told Adair that I was going to give her a chance to prove herself. Adair was African American so that motivated me to help her out. I knew they wouldn't allow her to progress in California, so I offered to send her overseas to Korea or Japan to referee. She admitted that she was afraid to fly. I remembered there was a match scheduled with a fighter from

Tijuana named Jorge "Maromero" Paez, dubbed the "Clown Prince" in Mexico City, Mexico. After speaking with Paez's manager they agreed to let Adair referee the fight. Adair wouldn't have to fly, she could take the train or bus to Tijuana.

Adair said she had the best experience of her life in Tijuana. When she arrived a crowd of women with flowers was waiting to welcome her in anticipation of refereeing the fight. She said Nacho Huizar, the promoter, rolled out the red carpet for her. She said the fight went well and congratulated me for the job that I had done. Because Gwen Adair wouldn't fly, there wasn't much that I could do to help her.

Jersey Joe and I added officials of various ethnicities to our roster. The IBF had calls from all over the country of people requesting referee positions. It wasn't long before we had our cadre of officials who were hired based on their skills. We recruited referees from many states including New York, Illinois, Florida, and California. We knew the time had come to integrate the commission. We felt that instead of fighters always getting banged up, they could be able to control the fight by being an official. Joe and I were proud that we gave people an opportunity where it otherwise might not have happened.

As the IBF president, I was able to send our officials all over the world. When we would send African Americans, people in England would tell them that they had never seen a Black referee or judge. We also gave opportunities to several women including Sheila Martin from Washington DC, Lynn Carter from Philly, and Eva Shain from Fort Lee, New Jersey. They too were sent around the world to officiate. I wanted people to understand how much we valued diversity, and Jersey Joe would seek out the best people without regard to color. Our officials weren't limited by borders, they traveled to Japan, Europe, South Africa, and Thailand to name a few. I too would enjoy visiting those exotic locations because the natives would greet me as though I was the greatest thing since popcorn. They weren't used to seeing a Black man with so much power. It was understood that I had the power to approve a fight and just as much power to stop one. However, when I wanted to spend more time at home, I would send my business partners. There would be complaints because the officials in those countries would want to see me. Most of the officials that we hired have now retired, but there are a few who continue to officiate.

CHAPTER 63

When traveling I didn't always look forward to those twenty-six-hour flights, but sometimes I had to buckle down and make the journey. I remember some of the Asian flights where the attendants were dressed in long flowing autumn-colored uniforms. The flight was bearable because they were so gracious and attentive. I often wondered if they thought I was part Asian because my last name is Lee. On one trip to Indonesia in 1985, a man and his wife were sitting across the aisle from me. He would strut around the cabin with an exaggerated view of himself like he was the big man on campus. The man held a folder that had his name and Assistant Secretary of Defense embossed on the front. My guess was he was a heavy hitter from Washington DC. When we deplaned the man and his wife headed toward customs. I was whisked right through to a waiting throng of reporters and television cameramen.

I was picked up at the airport in Surabaya, Indonesia by a man who had previously met with my son in my absence. The man called out my name as he approached me saying he was there to pick me up. He said that Mr. Aseng was outside waiting for my arrival. The man grabbed my bags and assured me that he would take care of them. My insulin was in my bag and it concerned me when he set the bags off to the side. He must have seen the look of concern on my face because he repeated that he was going to take care of them. Inside the terminal was a set of double doors and one flight attendant took my left arm and the other attendant took my right and led me through the doors. There was a sea of Asian fans cheering and saying my name as I entered with two beautiful women by my side. The crowd waved, took pictures, and shouted greetings and I thought to myself, "If the brothers could see me now."

I had to laugh at the gentleman who had been on the plane because now he was looking at me with an expression on his face that seemed to say who in the hell is he. Someone told the man who I was, he nodded respectfully in my direction. I gave him a quick nod as I mentally prepared for the "pressmins" that were being shoved around by the crowd as they jockeyed for an interview. I was preparing myself for a long day because once I left the airport Mr. Aseng said there would be a press conference at the hotel. He asked me if I needed to rest before attending and I told him that I was able to continue despite the thirteen-hour time difference. I was feeling rejuvenated and ready to take on the room full of reporters.

A beautiful Mercedes 600 pulled up complete with a chauffeur. Mr. Herry Sugiarto Aseng, my gracious host, said there were only two of those beauties in Indonesia. It was a beautiful car. When we arrived at the hotel, I noticed all the valet workers and attendants were saluting me. I must admit I enjoyed the attention; It was hard not to. I thought about how proud my mother would have been if she could have seen this with her own two eyes.

I was seated at the head table with the promoters during the luncheon. The question on everyone's mind was "Why Indonesia?" My speech was translated for the press and the story would be featured on their six o'clock news along with the footage of my arrival. I was once again offered the opportunity to get some rest, but I reminded them that my main purpose in Indonesia was to promote the event so that it would be successful. I assured them that I could wait a little longer before retiring to my quarters. Finally, after numerous interviews and socializing, we called it a night and I was shown to my room. The room was impressive especially the king-sized bed which I couldn't wait to dive into. I was told to be ready for lunch in one hour. I was thrilled that I would at least have time to shower and freshen up. The bed would have to wait.

The restaurant was on the fifteenth floor of a high-rise building. The restaurant was known for its Angus beef, a black beef at the top of the meat chain. Some of the best beef you can eat. Mr. Aseng couldn't speak English, so a translator was used to facilitate our discussion. As Mr. Aseng took me on a sightseeing tour, my eyes began to get a little heavy. It was time to rest. I was back at it after I had a few hours of sleep.

CHAPTER 64

The weigh-in for the fight happened later that day as Ellys Pical, a super flyweight known as "The Exocet", due to his powerful left hand and Ju Do Chun, IBF's Super Flyweight champion prepared for the fight. The people of Indonesia were ecstatic when Pical sent Chun to the canvas in the eighth round of the fight. Pical made history by becoming Indonesia's first world champion. The IBF made its mark in Indonesia.

When Japan, the Philippines, and Korea learned of my visit to Indonesia they made a special trip there to see if they could get the IBF to sponsor fights in their countries and utilize our officials. The trip to Indonesia opened doors in Southeast Asia for our federation. The time had come for me to return to the United States, but I decided to stay over a couple of days. Anything to delay taking the long flight home. Going from east to west wasn't too bad, but jet lag took over when going west to east. Once I got back to New Jersey I slept for nearly three days.

CHAPTER 65

A fighter from Korea named Chong Pal Park, a 168-pound fighter, was the best in the world. He was an IBF fighter who knocked out anyone who stepped into the ring with him. Chong decided to move to a heavier weight and another federation, these are decisions he would come to regret. Chong got knocked out in his next fight and never recovered. His boxing career came to an end. There were a few IBF champions that hailed from the Philippines and Thailand, but during those days the Koreans were better fighters because they tended to be stronger.

My name became a household word in Southeast Asia. A promoter out of Surabaya, Indonesia, Mr. Aseng, owned two large printing presses and was the only person who could supply the printing needs of mainland China. He was fond of me as I discovered through our translator, because of my chubbiness. He said it showed prosperity. I thought it showed that I needed to lay off the pizza pies. Mr. Aseng said the first time he saw me I was wearing a red tie and handkerchief and the Chinese love red. It is a color of good fortune. Mr. Aseng told the people of China that it was their best bet to get involved in boxing. I made several trips to Indonesia even though I didn't want to. I went because Yang would summon me for help. He was concerned that the new commissioner might minimize my presence in boxing in China. He wanted me to remain influential in Asia.

I was invited to an event that Mr. Aseng said was an hour-long drive from the Indonesian airport. At the celebration, people were dancing, eating, and having a great time. I made a speech to the crowd at the request of Mr. Aseng. The new commissioner came to the stage and put his arm around Mr. Aseng and announced him as the official promoter of most of the fights that were to be held in Indonesia. The commissioner and I became friendly with each other, he even attended the IBF convention in

Toronto, Canada. We didn't have the same type of success in Japan, several obstacles were blocking an alliance with them, namely, them being in bed with the WBC. We just went around the Japanese since we couldn't get through to them.

CHAPTER 66

The IBF encountered many obstacles while hosting various fights throughout the United States. Many of the challenges that I faced as president of the IBF may have been occasioned because the hue of my skin is darker than those who were making major decisions. They would rather go outside of the country to do business than to help contribute to the success of a Black man who opened doors for the less fortunate and disenfranchised.

It was challenging for American fighters once they left the country. I saw nationalism in full effect when traveling around the world. The WBC which was headquartered in Central America tended to favor the Mexican fighters. The WBA favored Venezuelans' and South Americans. With the IBF being the new kids on the block, we had to prove to the world that American boxers deserved their place in the ring.

Although Jersey Joe and I began to make a name for ourselves in the boxing game throughout the United States, we were remembered for making Newark, New Jersey the "Jewel of the East Coast" for boxing. We became known as the duo who opened doors for several fighters, promoters, managers, and trainers. We also worked closely with the networks and the casinos. I began making personal appearances around the country promoting the IBF. Bill Brennan, our Championship Chairman, Vice Presidents: James Stevenson of Louisiana, Alvin Goodman of Florida, Hiawatha Knight of Michigan, and Mike Cusimano of Louisiana were sent out to different countries to spread the IBF's message of fairness, brotherhood, and success. They were instructed to monitor some of the fights that our organization was involved in. We were well received in other countries because of the way we conducted business. This made them gravitate toward the IBF. This appeared to have angered the WBA and WBC.

Don King informed me that he didn't want to work with the IBF because of his long-standing relationship with the Latinos. He wanted to remain in good standing with them. I told King that I wasn't asking for 100% of his business, we only wanted him to give us as much consideration as he would the other two federations. I also had a discussion with Bob Arum in which I asked him to cooperate with the IBF whenever he fought in Atlantic City. Arum said he would see what he could do. Eventually, the other federations gravitated toward the IBF because they had champions that they weren't sure what to do with. We had several vacancies and they decided that they would let some of their boxers fight for the openings. They soon discovered that the IBF had stronger, more intensive fighters than the other federations. The IBF was starting to make progress, but it was an uphill battle with numerous obstacles trying to halt our success. I was determined that we would persevere and move forward with the organization.

CHAPTER 67

The fighter from South Africa, Welcome Ncita, also known as "The Hawk", finally got his opportunity to fight for the IBF against bantamweight Fabrice Benichou. Cedric Kushner, known as being one of the most significant promoters of boxing, decided to promote the fight in Tel Aviv, Israel, which was new territory for the IBF. The fight was to be held in March of 1990. Tel Aviv was neutral ground for fighters and acquiring this match was looked upon as a great accomplishment for the IBF. Ncita won the title and became the champion for his weight class. The Ncita-Benichou match opened doors for our organization because promoters felt that since the IBF promoted their fighters, they should support their federation.

Apartheid was slowly being dismantled which meant more fights were scheduled to take place in South Africa. Our annual conference was scheduled to be held in New Orleans, Louisiana and they approached me to interview at a local radio station. They informed me that Al Sharpton would be in attendance during the interview to discuss my opinion on apartheid. It was well known that Sharpton had taken a hard stance on dealing with South Africa. Sharpton believed the IBF should take the same position and blackball anything having to do with South Africa.

I explained to Sharpton that a young man who looked like me asked for a chance to box. I couldn't tell him no. From the bus boycotts in Montgomery to the sit-ins at Woolworths, we understood how it felt to want equal rights. I explained to the radio host and Sharpton that we had all drank from the bitter cup of racism and they both should understand my position on giving this young fighter a chance. I argued that this young man had no control over the apartheid policies of his government. Ncita won the title and the IBF supported him, but we refused to allow the fight to take place in South Africa. This young man has now opened the door for other boxers in his homeland to compete. I asked Sharpton wasn't this Dr. King's, Roy Wilkins, and E. Phillip Randolph's intention, to open the door for the disenfranchised? I told Sharpton that I didn't expect him to condemn me. I felt the two of us should link arms and work together to further the equal rights agenda.

Sharpton refused to back down on his criticism of the IBF. The radio host said she couldn't understand Sharpton's position because he knew African Americans have been through this same type of discrimination. It appeared that Sharpton was trying to stop progress. Unhappy with the direction of the interview Sharpton said he didn't agree with my beliefs and there would be people, particularly in the New York area, that would condemn us for our relationship with South Africa.

Al Sharpton mentioned a man by the name of Randall Robinson, head of a Pan African organization who planned to come down hard on the IBF for conducting business with South Africa. Al finished the interview, shook my hand, and said he would see me back in the city. With Sharpton in Brooklyn and me in Jersey, we knew we would run into each other again.

I returned to the hotel to conduct an IBF business meeting. As I am speaking, a man comes in to say that there is a picket line protest outside the hotel. I asked the man who was leading the march and he said, Al Sharpton. I went outside to see the protest and was surprised by what I saw. It appeared that Sharpton had gathered and paid several homeless people to be a part of the protest. It was almost comical. I just shook my head and returned to the meeting.

CHAPTER 68

Our banquet was scheduled for later that night. As we prepared to enjoy our meal and listen to the musical entertainment, the music director informed me that Al Sharpton and a guest were trying to enter the banquet hall. I was asked if it was okay to allow Sharpton to enter, or should the police be called to arrest the two of them. This could easily be done in the south. I instructed the man to allow Sharpton and his guest to enter if they paid for their tickets, but if they tried to bring any nonsense into the event he would be forcefully removed. Sharpton paid for the tickets. My nephew and two of his muscular friends, who were itching for a confrontation, stood behind me as I approached Sharpton. Their stance made it clear that no foolishness would be accepted. I ask Al how he was doing and replied that he was doing well. I told him that I was surprised to see him, especially after the radio interview earlier that day.

Al seemed surprised that he was almost denied access to the banquet. I explained that they thought he was going to start trouble, but if he came in peace, he was more than welcome to attend the event. I told him if he started a commotion during the banquet, they wouldn't hesitate to summon the police and have him removed. Al promised not to cause any problems and was so quiet and low key that guests barely knew he was in attendance. Sharpton knew that the people attending the conference were not interested in his rhetoric.

The convention ended after a few awards were distributed. The next day, I flew back to New Jersey. Upon my return, I was informed by Don King and Al Sharpton that King sent Sharpton to the banquet and paid for his ticket for the express purpose of disrupting it. I laughed and told him that he didn't do a very good job and Al agreed. King said due to his opposition to apartheid, he decided to send Al to the banquet to teach the

IBF a lesson. I told Sharpton that I was glad he knew better than to go through with it. This was another instance when the stars were lined up in my favor, it would have been embarrassing to have that type of disruption during our convention. I told Sharpton that I couldn't believe he would attempt to sabotage my event. I reminded King that the WBA has officers from South Africa, and the two of them don't say a word and continue to do business with their organization. King said you must take it where you can get it. If you have champions you have to deal with them. I told King that a circle is round. What goes around comes right back around.

The IBF continued to progress and gain popularity in the boxing arena. Although I didn't actively seek out Don King for his business, he had a few champions that were looking for somewhere to fight. Walter Stone told King to allow his boxers to fight for the IBF title. King said that he was close to the other guys and didn't want them to think that he had jumped ship. Stone reminded King that he had enough fighters that he could work with all three federations. He said there was enough for everybody. Nobody had to be selfish or greedy. Don King finally gave in and agreed to promote fights with the IBF.

CHAPTER 69

Before running for the WBA presidency, and while I was still with the State Athletic Commission in New Jersey, King wanted to promote a fight at the Playboy Hotel and Casino in Atlantic City. He had to go through the IBF in order to make it happen. We gave King permission since he had a license to promote in New Jersey and we knew he would have Frank Gelb assist him in putting on the fight.

The main event was to take place on March 20, 1982, between Floyd "Jumbo Cummings out of Chicago and Larry Frazier from Seattle, Washington. The weigh-in was held the night before the match. The fight was slated to air on CBS television at one o'clock pm EST. Jumbo was a former inmate of Stateville Correctional Center, where he had been incarcerated for several years on a murder charge. During his time in prison, he strengthened his body and had muscles protruding from every part of his body. When Jumbo stepped on the scale surrounded by photographers and reporters, he looked like a powerhouse. When Larry stepped on the scale, they began to mean mug each other. Both boxers were about the same height, 6'3, but Jumbo weighed slightly more than Larry. The fighters posed for pictures and were told to report to their dressing rooms the next day around noon to change, get their hands wrapped, and prepare to go into the ring. The fighters had to be ready when the television producer called so that the television station didn't go black waiting for the fight to begin.

As everyone anticipated the start of the fight one of the inspectors approached me in a panic. He told me that I needed to get down to the dressing room immediately. I asked him what the urgency was. He said they were unable to locate Frazier. I asked if they checked his dressing room. The inspector said that was the first place they looked. I asked if he had spoken with Larry's manager, Mike "Motormouth" Morton, he said he hadn't been able to reach him either. As I walked to the dressing room area, I ran into Don King and he told me that I needed to make something happen really quick. He said the event was about to fall apart, which means he was about to lose the CBS and casino money. I asked what was going on and King replied that they couldn't find Frazier. I began searching for him, asking people if they had seen him. Several men said they hadn't seen Frazier since the previous night. I tried to remain calm while searching for Larry. I knew that my only responsibility was to make sure the fight took place. If we couldn't find Frazier, we would call in a replacement.

Finally, Morton arrived and approached me saying that he'd found Frazier. I told Morton to have Frazier get to his dressing room so that he could prepare for the fight. Morton said that would be a little difficult because Frazier was back in Seattle. I yelled at Morton asking why Frazier was in Seattle, instead of being here in Atlantic City. Morton said after the weigh-in Frazier waited until everyone was asleep, went into his room, took both of their airline tickets, and flew back to Seattle. He is refusing to fight. I asked Morton how he knew this information, and he said Frazier contacted him from Seattle. King became enraged and started yelling about not trusting the fighters. I tried to calm King by offering to send in a replacement for Frazier. Eventually, King consented to a replacement but wanted to make sure Larry Frazier would have serious consequences for skipping out on his match. I assured King that Frazier would be under suspension for failure to appear and not honoring his contract. The fight took place with both fighters being replaced. Neither Frazier or Jumbo fought that night.

A few days later Joe and I received a call from Larry Frazier apologizing for bailing out on us. He said that he knew that he wasn't prepared to fight Jumbo, especially on television. I asked Larry if he realized the predicament that he put everyone in. I explained that we had to fudge our way through awkward interviews. Frazier asked for an opportunity to come before the board to explain why he bailed. I asked him what made him decide to contact me. Frazier said his mother was home when he got back to Seattle and asked him what he was doing home. She said that he should be fighting in Atlantic City. Larry tried to explain to his mother that his heart wasn't into fighting Jumbo. His mother told him that she had a house full of her church members over to watch the fight knowing her son would be a part of the main event on television. His mother said that she was embarrassed that she had to tell all those people that her son wasn't fighting. Frazier said his mother went up and down his back like a window shade. He said he wished he had fought Jumbo because what he had to endure from his mother was far worse than what Jumbo would have done to him. I told Larry I would let him know the date of the hearing. I said that I expected him to show up and he was more than welcome to bring an attorney.

On the day of the hearing Larry showed up without an attorney and Joe and I had an opportunity to interview him. As the commissioner, Jersey Joe had the final decision on his punishment which would be enacted on the state level. This decision would also be carried out throughout the country. Joe asked Frazier what happened. Larry said he freaked out when he saw the massive body on Jumbo Cummings and feared that Jumbo would defeat him. That's why he grabbed the airline tickets and went home. Frazier said that he received more harassment from his mother then he would have if he had lost the fight to Cummings. Frazier asked to have his suspension cut short so that he could return to the ring and make it up to her. I had never really seen Jersey Joe angry, but that day was a different story. Joe told Frazier that as a heavyweight he carries the ball for boxing. The way they go so goes boxing. Joe told him that he was supposed to be on national television and fight for a sold-out crowd, but you walked away from a fight. Joe asked him if he realized how bad he made everybody look. He said Larry is a part of a fraternity as a heavyweight fighter and instead of you standing up to Jumbo, you kicked the can down the road. Joe told Larry he didn't know what to do with him. Frazier tried to explain to Joe that he didn't mean anything by leaving, that he just got caught up in the moment. Joe told Larry that he was upset that he didn't have the decency to inform the promoter, Bob Lee, or him so that a replacement could have been found. Larry claimed that he didn't think about it. He said all he thought about was getting back home, but when he went home, he ran into a storm; his mother.

Joe dismissed Larry and had him wait in the next room while we decided what we were going to do. The IBF members analyzed the extent of the damage caused by Frazier's absence, eventually deciding to have

Frazier honor the contract between him and Don King to fight Jumbo Cummings within 90 days. If Larry refused, he would be suspended indefinitely. We called Frazier back into the room and read him the riot act before informing him of the outcome. Jersey Joe asked me to call Don King to let him know of the agreement so that he could begin promoting the Frazier-Cummings fight.

King ranted over the phone still angry with Frazier for costing him so much money. Don King finally calmed down and said that he would go along with the IBF's decision. King decided to move the fight to Ohio. The fight was held at Stouffers Ballroom in Cleveland on August 14, 1982. The public was excited once the rematch was announced. Larry defeated Jumbo in the tenth round. That's when I realized that weightlifters don't make successful boxers. They are good at lifting weights, hitting baseballs, and playing football, because their muscles tend to lock up. Jumbo couldn't stop Frazier's left jab and he didn't have the dexterity that boxers need to be successful. Larry Frazier could now go back home and face his mother.

CHAPTER 70

When the casinos in Atlantic City opened their doors to boxing, Atlantic City became a popular place to host boxing matches. They began to attract more promoters and fighters, especially after the entertainment promoter Frank Gelb began to help promoters with their boxing matches. He was known as the man who could get things done. During the baseball strike in 1981, many people began to migrate towards boxing. There would be as many as three fights each week on network television. One on Tuesday, one Thursday, and one during the weekend. All the networks were involved including HBO.

CHAPTER 71

My one and only son, Robert Lee Jr., was born in 1961. He was five years old when his mother and I divorced and she and my children moved to East Orange, New Jersey. I maintained a home for them in Scotch Plains so they could visit whenever they wanted. After six months in East Orange, my son asked if he could return to Scotch Plains to live with me. I was happy to have him come back home. My parents and my sister were always there to help me with Robert Jr., I don't know what I would have done without them. When he would come home from school my mother would be at my house ready to feed him and help with his homework. She watched over her grandson like a mother hen.

It was important for me to help my son with his studies. I remember struggling with Robert Jr. on the so-called "new math". It became such a headache I told him we were going back to the basics. When it was time for parent-teacher conferences I realized that his teacher was married to a friend of mine. I attended their wedding. I arrived early and sat in on their math lesson. The teacher wrote a problem on the chalkboard for the students to solve. Eight or more of the students attempted unsuccessfully to solve the problem. Robert Jr. volunteered to solve the problem using the "old school" method that I taught him at home. The teacher praised him for his success at the board. I was so proud of my son. During the conference, I explained to the teacher how I had helped my son with his math. To my dismay, she said that they didn't want parents working with their children on the math problems. She said they wanted the students to figure the problems out on their own. I was taken aback by her statement. I reminded her that none of the other students were successful at solving the problem that she presented on the board. She continued to stand by her previous statement. That was the day that I lost respect for his teacher, or at least the way she taught her class. From that day forward, I told my son to show me his work before turning it in to ensure that it was correct.

I was proud of my son because he ended up being a model student and athlete. He played football, baseball, and basketball, and excelled in all three. When Robert Jr. graduated, he was among the top six percent of African American students nationwide. He applied to Stanford University but was denied. He eventually attended Pittsburg University, where he received a partial scholarship, I covered the remaining balance. Robert Jr. became homesick and decided not to return to Pitt after completing his first year. I believe that he was bored at Pitt because there wasn't a lot of action to keep him entertained on campus. I expressed my disappointment to my son for not returning to school. He said that he thought that I would be pleased that he wasn't going to continue throwing my money away by not applying himself to his studies. He said that he just couldn't take it anymore. Upon Robert Jr's return to New Jersey, he went to work alongside his mother at Bell Telephone and was very successful.

CHAPTER 72

My daughter Cheryl Ann Lee was born on August 4, 1965. Around the age of two, Cheryl became ill. At that time, I had been divorced for nearly two years from her mother. Her mother tried to figure out what was ailing Cheryl but to no avail. Eventually, Cheryl was seen by an Italian pediatrician named Dr. Palumbo who had a reputation for being knowledgeable in the medical field, and his office was in Scotch Plains. He diagnosed Cheryl with Sickle Cell Anemia. Not long after the diagnosis, she had a stroke that affected her brain development. This caused her to have challenges when she was in elementary school. She often required extra help, but she managed to make it through high school. After she graduated, she began working for me at IBF after having difficulties finding a job.

I twisted my ankle during an evening walk. My primary physician referred me to an orthopedic doctor. After reading my X-rays the doctor told me that my ankle was fractured. He said half of my leg would need to be amputated. I told him I was going to get a second opinion, and I quickly exited his office. Having my leg cut off didn't fit into my plans. There was an African American doctor who worked in our building named Jim Lee. He found out through my son about my ailment and reached out to me. I was frantic as I told him the previous doctor's diagnosis. Jim Lee said he wasn't going to cut off my leg, but he would have to operate on it. I was flat on my back as I recuperated from my surgery.

CHAPTER 73

Robert Jr and Cheryl both worked for me at the IBF while I was on the mend. Harold Smith reemerged after completing his obligation to the government, and once again began promoting boxing. It was odd, but the fact that Smith had swindled a large amount of money seemed to draw others to him. Getting people to work with him didn't seem to be a problem. Harold started helping with the boxing shows. He had contacts in China who wanted him to come there and assist with boxing events.

Harold called me while I was still in the hospital and said that he had a big fight coming off in Beijing, China and he needed me to come to give the event some authenticity. I told him that I would, but I was laid up in the hospital with my leg in a cast. He asked if there was anyone else that I could send as a representative for the IBF. I told him I would send my namesake, Robert Jr., to represent the IBF. Harold said he would call me back and let me know if they were willing to accept my replacement. When Harold called back, he said they would welcome my son as a stand-in, and he could bring a guest all expenses paid. I asked if it would be okay if my daughter attended with her brother, and he said that would be okay. He asked me to send him their information so that he could make their travel arrangements. My son also took his girlfriend along.

Although It wasn't an IBF fight my son was given the royal treatment. They introduced him during the boxing match and later took him and my daughter sightseeing. They took pictures, but China is a security conscience place. There were restrictions on the number of pictures that you could take and where you could take them, so you had to be cautious when snapping pictures. Cheryl was on the Great Wall of China, a place that I've never been to, taking pictures, but no one bothered her. My son said they provided transportation to get around to see the sights, so Cheryl would call the front desk and tell them to have the driver pick her up at ten o'clock in front of the building, in her most proper dialect. She was having a great time. Now I'm not one to brag, but my daughter was beautiful, and she stood around 5'10 and towered over the people in China.

When it was time to pass through Customs, everyone was reminded that it is illegal to take any type of fruit out of China. Everyone followed directions except for Cheryl who was being stubborn. She had a banana in her purse. Cheryl was taken into a room and searched. They were serious about her taking the fruit because had my son not paid the 126 dollars fine, they would have kept Cheryl over there. My son warned Cheryl that he was going to tell me about her little faux pas, and she knew that I would give her a hard time. She got off easy because I was sitting with a cast on my leg and didn't have the energy to fuss with her. I did tell her that she went all the way over to China to get in trouble over a raggedy banana. I told her that she should have eaten the banana. Robert Jr. was pleased with the hospitality and accommodations that Harold Smith provided. This information let me know that I would be there if Smith ever needed me. Harold Smith disappeared from the boxing scene and I never heard from him again. Did his past transgressions catch up to him or did he decide to give up on boxing? No one knew for sure.

Cheryl began to submit applications to different companies in New Jersey. A woman who faced the same challenges as my daughter told Cheryl about a position with the government. She was given a test that she passed with flying colors, and she was hired to work for the Department of Defense. One of the perks of the position was the location. It was close to Scotch Plains where Cheryl lived. I was a proud papa seeing my daughter striking out on her own.

CHAPTER 74

In May of 1988, I was working on my wife's car, removing an oil filter and twisted it so hard that the tendon jumped off my middle finger. I couldn't straighten it out. My doctor referred me to an orthopedic doctor in Plainfield. He told me that he needed to operate on the tendon. My primary doctor informed me that while I was under anesthesia, he noticed some irregularities in my heart. I was referred to a cardiologist for a consultation. The cardiologist sent me to JFK Hospital in New Brunswick, New Jersey to have pictures taken of my heart. They sent me to Beth Israel Medical Center in Newark, New Jersey for an evaluation. I was told by Dr. Hussein, a member of the medical staff, that I had at least four blockages in my heart. I asked the doctor if my condition was severe. The doctor said that I could walk out of his office and drop dead on the sidewalk, or I could ignore the condition and live another 20-30 years. He said he couldn't say for sure, but eventually, it needed to be taken care of.

I asked Dr. Hussein how soon he would be able to perform the surgery. He said that it would be a go as soon as he cleared it with my primary physician. I entered Beth Israel on September 13, 1988. I was told that once they opened me up, they realized that not only were arteries one and two clogged, so were three and four. This meant a quadruple heart bypass surgery. They did some new-fangled procedure where they took a vein from my leg and used it in my heart. I was glad they didn't use a vein from a pig. A common practice at the time.

Robert Jr. asked me about working in my place at the IBF. Although I liked the idea, I wasn't sure how well it would be received having my son take over my position. He explained that he was accustomed to dealing with people and he was sure that he could handle the IBF staff. I called my secretary and asked her to add Robert Jr. to the payroll.

Robert Jr. was a quick learner and he was my eyes and my ears during my absence, which was his main purpose for joining the organization. With the addition of Robert Jr. came jealousy with some of the staff saying that my son was receiving preferential treatment. I saw it as a father looking out for his son's best interest. I sent my son on trips around the far east, but they were always disappointed because they were looking for me to be there. They would accept Robert Jr. because they knew that he represented me. I would tell them that I would be back in action as soon as I was well.

I was sidelined for over two months while I recovered. I had to make a few modifications around the house so that I could go up and down the stairs. While I was recovering the IBF headquarters moved, and the location had stairs. My secretary had a lift installed before I returned to the office. Shortly after I returned to work the IBF moved again to East Orange, New Jersey. Fortunately, this location had stairs and an elevator.

My son learned a lot about the business by being around Arum, King, Lewis, Muhammad, and Lou Duva and he was quite capable of handling the position his father entrusted to him. His professionalism allowed me to recuperate without worrying about the direction of the IBF. Robert Jr. demonstrated his worth when he opened doors for the IBF in South Africa.

I decided to add my nephew Darryl Peoples to oversee ratings, due to the current ratings chairman Doug Beavers needing to step away from his post. The IBF could no longer retain him. Darryl was highly efficient when it came to the ratings, and that is why I put him in charge. I put Robert Jr. in charge of championships. Some people began to question Robert Jr. being on the payroll, but I was looking to create a legacy much like the Kennedy and Bush families. There is nothing wrong with taking care of your own. I knew if I couldn't trust anyone else, I could definitely trust my family. I believe you should surround yourself with your kinfolk as long as they can do the job. Hiring my son was a strategic move, he was an extension of me. I planned to groom my son with the expectation that he would one day take over as leader of the IBF. I wanted to secure his future as many successful people had done with their children.

CHAPTER 75

The IBF was gaining ground and beginning to gain attention from the media and the boxing community. Boxing champions began to gravitate toward us because they knew they would get a fair shake. Many of the fighters felt that they were more likely to have someone who looks like them look out for their best interest. There was also the fact that everyone admired Jersey Joe Walcott, the international boxing commissioner.

The IBF was being built into a business-like organization that was being run like any business on Madison or Fifth Avenue. Our doors opened promptly at 9 am sharp and remained open until 5 pm. I refused to have our organization viewed as lazy or unprofessional. I demanded an efficient office with professional staff. We always manned the phones during our office hours to accommodate our clients, no matter which country they may have been calling from. However, there were instances when time knew no boundaries when officials from other countries would contact me directly without regard to the time zone, I was available to handle business. If a promoter wanted to schedule a championship bout, they usually needed an immediate response. It was commonplace to receive calls at two, three, four o'clock in the morning. The IBF was global, something that was understood by the entire staff. We dealt with different nationalities, languages, and time zones, and we were accommodating to all of them.

As the IBF rolled out the welcome mat for the promoters, boxers, and people in the boxing community, we worked to become an international organization. We achieved this by having people from other countries play a role in our organization. We had a young fighter from Chicago, Illinois by the name of Joe Louis Manley, he was a junior welterweight champion having won the title from Howard Davis Jr. in February 1986. Manley was preparing to defend his title and there was a young boxer from England named Terry Marsh who challenged him.

We agreed to have the bout in London, England. I was invited to attend the fight along with the people that I assigned to the match. The sponsor of the fight was Frank Warren. He was a secondary promoter to Mickey Duff who was the main promoter coming out of England through the British Boxing Board of Patrol. They were the ones in charge of boxing in Britain. Frank wanted to promote the fight because he saw Terry as a capable adversary for Manley. Stan Hoffman, Manley's manager, was also eager to put the fight on. Holding it in England added an international flavor.

The fight commenced with the officials that we helped assign. The fight was evenly matched for a while, but as the fight went on, we could see that Marsh had the advantage over Manley. Marsh was able to overcome anything that Manley threw his way. In the end, Marsh won the fight with a TKO. As the fight ended Manley took a nosedive and became unconscious. They rushed him to the dressing room to see if he needed medical attention, and I went to see how he was doing. We ended up having the London officials guide us to the hospital. We wanted to be sure it wasn't anything too serious. We found out that it was nothing to do with the head, it had more to do with the body. He had been banged up pretty good and was dehydrated. They wanted to keep him overnight for observation. We told them to hold on to him and once he got better, we would come and escort him back to the United States.

During that time there was a man by the name of Jon Robinson who was a boxing guru. He liked to go to all the fights and be involved, but he somehow offended the powers in the British Boxing Board. They didn't want anything to do with him. When we got ready to take Manley to the hospital Jon offered his assistance. He called for a taxi so that we could follow Manly to the hospital. He knew that I was at a disadvantage being in a foreign country and some things must be done a little differently than in the US. I went along with Jon and after everything settled down, he offered to become our England and European representative. He informed us that he didn't get along with the British Boxing Board. I asked him why. He said they had a long-standing feud between them because he had been somewhat outspoken and critical of some of the things that they had done, so he had fallen into disfavor with them. He went on to say that he had a desire to work for the IBF for several years, and he would love to be our European contact. I told him that I would give it some thought and reach out to him once I returned to the United States.

We wrapped up everything in London and returned to the United States with Terry Marsh being our first European champion. Marsh ended up having a falling out with his promoter Frank Warren. The next thing I knew someone was accused of trying to shoot Frank Warren at the airport. They accused Terry Marsh. I thought that was a strange kettle of fish. Terry Marsh later became ill and went to the hospital for a while. He may have fought once or twice after that, but his illness prevented him from representing England as our champion for any length of time.

CHAPTER 76

Tony Sibson, who had been fighting on the world scene for quite a while, wanted to challenge Frank Tate for the middleweight championship. Stan Hoffman was Frank Tate's manager, and he was a promoter in Houston, Texas. The two got together in England intending to have a fifteen-round fight for the middleweight title. Frank Warren ran into a hail storm with the British Boxing Board because the WBA and WBC didn't agree with our policy of having fifteen round bouts. They felt like a fighter was more likely to be seriously hurt if a fight lasted more than twelve rounds. They went back and forth as to whether the fight was going to take place. Warren called me and asked me to come to London and discuss this matter with the British Boxing Board because he wanted the fight to go on, and he wanted Sibson to get a chance to fight for the title.

They arranged my transportation to England and upon my arrival. I had a meeting with Superior Court Justice Sir David Hopkins. Frank Warren, Justice Hopkins, and I had a sit-down and discussed the controversy of twelve rounds versus fifteen. Many great fights throughout the years went fifteen rounds, and I believed there were other things that challenged the safety of fighters aside from the number of rounds of a fight. I had a convincing argument as to why we should be permitted to have a fifteen-round fight, and how it would benefit Sibson if he were to become the champion. Hopkins started his argument against fifteen rounds saying the IBF would be isolated because we were the only federation that allowed fifteen rounds. Hopkins said the other federations would take advantage of the IBF and run bouts in their jurisdiction that the IBF wouldn't be able to participate in. He said that he wasn't siding with anyone, he was doing what was best for the sport.

Hopkins asked me to allow the fight between Sibson and Tate to go for twelve rounds, and I could decide if I wanted to continue using a fifteen-round format. Hopkins said the fight was scheduled to be aired on NBC television from England to the United States and wanted people to know that our world-class organization would be a part of it. He explained that he wanted our organization to be consistent with the other organizations and he knew the other two federations weren't going to budge on this issue. I told him that I would give him my answer in the morning. Hopkins said he hoped that common sense would prevail, and we would put this fight on. He said that all of England wants to see Sibson fight, and Sibson wanted to fight, he didn't care how many rounds he fought. My main goal was the longevity of our organization.

Frank and I went to lunch to discuss the fight. He told me the ball was in my court, he said he would go along with whatever I decided. After going back and forth on the pros and cons of twelve versus fifteen rounds, I told Frank that I would mull it over and give him my decision in the morning. I thought about it and I knew that I didn't want to shoot myself in the foot and lose the support of the people who helped us on the international level. I had to determine the way the wind was blowing, it appeared to be blowing toward twelve round matches. I decided the IBF would try out twelve rounds on a trial basis because that's what the promoters and commissioners desired. I figured it wasn't the worst thing that could happen. I had to let my common sense prevail and allow the fight to proceed with only twelve rounds. I informed them of my decision to allow the fight to be televised on American television the next day and to follow the other federations with a twelve-round bout. I didn't look at it as a defeat, but a decision that was in the best interest of the IBF.

When I returned to the U.S. and discussed it with the executive committee, they agreed. We realized if we didn't go with twelve rounds, we could lose out on fights that would be shown on HBO or other television stations. We did what we had to do to survive.

CHAPTER 77

Just before the fight started someone let off a firebomb in the arena. I wasn't sure if it was in protest of the fight, or if someone was trying to get attention, but it held the fight up for quite a while. There were a couple of former fighters from England who addressed the crowd and told whoever was causing the confusion to stop with the shenanigans and to allow the fight to proceed. The fighters reminded the crowd that this wasn't the way they did things in England. Whoever tossed the firebomb must have calmed down because there were no more issues during the fight.

I used Jon Robinson's services as one of our assistants in Europe and England. He was an asset to our organization, but he had a very bombastic manner when doing business and he angered a lot of people. One of the people he worked with from Italy named Benedetto Montella was recruited by Jon to be a judge for some of the matches. They worked well together until Jon decided he wanted to branch out and create his own organization. He wanted to be his own boss because he had his own ideas of how to lead. My way was different than his, I believe you use honey not vinegar to get bees. He used vinegar and it just didn't work.

The IBF recruited Benedetto Montella to replace Jon Robinson once he started his own organization called the World Boxing Union. Adding Montella to our roster turned out to be a smart move because he was a travel agent who spoke several languages fluently. He did business in Greece, Germany, Spain, and France. He was an asset to our organization. I always say when the good Lord closes one door, he opens another one. He brought Benedetto to us just as Jon was leaving.

Montella created a great deal of activity in Europe, particularly in Italy and France which helped us be more of an international entity. He was instrumental in securing the IBF fight in Tel Aviv, Israel, where Fabrice Benichou lost to Welcome Ncita.

There was another place near the Canary Islands where we had a fighter named Taginesta. He came to Italy and won a title and took it back to the island. My wife and I were invited by the Prime Minister from Spain to take a trip to the Canary Islands. The islands were owned by the Spaniards. We flew from the United States to Madrid and from there we flew to the Canary Islands. Our plane ride took us across the spectacular Mediterranean Sea, the scenery was beautiful. This was indeed the playground for the rich and famous. We spent about five days there, hanging on by a shoestring. With the luxurious hotels, sand, and sun, it was some kind of beautiful. The guy that met us there was driving a Bentley, a car that was over 200,000 dollars. They showed us around and took us to a fancy restaurant and tourist attractions. We were traveling first class. We had a meeting with the Prime Minister, and then we met some officials in the Canary Islands. We were able to put another feather in our cap for reaching out to a distant country. It broadened our base.

We had an interesting situation occur in the French Riviera in Monte Carlo where Prince Ranier and Princess Grace resided. They had a casino that they wanted to bring in additional entertainment for people to enjoy while they gambled. My wife and I had been there once before on an excursion from the United States and we stayed at Lowes Monte Carlo. It was a beautiful hotel and we had first-class accommodations. This time we returned to Monte Carlo for the boxing match. Cedric Kushner had an agreement with Benedetto Montella to put on a show in Monte Carlo. The match was scheduled for October 19, 1985, between Chisanda Mutti from Zambia and Lee Roy Murphy out of Chicago. Kushner was Murphy's promoter. the fight was taking place with the help of Montella. We flew into Nice, which is along the Mediterranean and took ground transportation into Monte Carlo. As we went to the hotel, we saw the magnificent ships, the harbors, and the stunning landscape.

CHAPTER 78

I had to assign the officials for the fight. Larry Hazzard was the referee who would soon become the commissioner of New Jersey. I selected Hazzard because he was one of the best and I wanted to put my best foot forward. I also assigned Lorenzo Casentini from Italy and Norbert Hansen from Norway. There was another guy from Switzerland, but his name escapes me. We had the weigh-in for the fight with the bout scheduled for 8 pm. There weren't as many spectators in attendance as they predicted. A few boxing buffs, a few stragglers, and a few people looking to be entertained made for a decent crowd.

The two fighters were evenly matched, but Murphy was a better fighter. Around the twelfth round, something happened that I had never seen before and haven't seen since. Both fighters threw right hands at the same time. It seemed as if their hands moved in slow motion. They hit the floor at the same time. Hazzard knew just what to do. He positioned himself between both fighters and began the count on both fighters. When he reached eight, Murphy pulled himself up on the ropes. Hazzard continued counting to ten for Mutti since he was still on the floor. Murphy won the fight by a knockout. The crowd howled at the outcome because they had never seen such an ending. The cameras were rolling, and Kushner was running around the ring screaming for the photographers to get the picture. He wanted the picture to put out on the Associated Press wire. When Hazzard called the fight over and raised Lee Roy Murphy's hand, everyone cheered, not because of who won but because of the unusual outcome. The Murphy-Mutti fight was one to remember.

We packed, went to our rooms, and prepared to leave. We had to take a tram that carried about thirty passengers including the boxers from the night before. I took a seat and when I looked up, I noticed Lee Roy Murphy standing in front of me holding on to a pole. He said that he hoped I enjoyed myself because apparently it was a good fight. I asked him what he meant by apparently. He confessed that the last thing he remembered until this morning was Mutti's right hand coming straight for him at the same time he was throwing his right hand. He said he didn't recall what happened, and when he went down his corner told him that he grabbed the ropes and pulled himself up to retain his title. He said he was out like a light. Murphy said they went to get a bite to eat, but he had no idea that he had won the fight. I told him when he got back to Chicago to go to his doctor to make sure he didn't have a concussion. He said that was the first thing he was going to do.

When we got back to the states, Murphy was still a little shaky. I told his trainer to make sure he takes it easy for a while. Although Murphy had other fights, I never saw him again. I was grateful that this fight played a role in helping the IBF advance in the international market, and with the publicity of the double-knock-out, the IBF would receive plenty of publicity.

CHAPTER 79

Another interesting event happened in South Korea. I took my wife with me on this trip. A fighter Suh Sung In from Korea was fighting against Bobby Berna from the Philippines on December 4, 1983. We conducted the weigh-in and everybody introduced themselves. It was an international match-up. There is a rule in boxing, if one fighter is cut by a punch and he is behind on the points, he loses by a technical decision. If there is a head butt and he is behind on points, he loses on a technical decision. The guy who does the butting wins the fight, only if it is determined the head butt was an accident. I took a referee with me by the name of Joe Cortez, who was the referee over the main event.

There was a large crowd with standing room only. Everyone was cheering for their native son Sung In. As they got to the ninth round Berna hit Sung In with a left and split his eye open. The crowd thought that Sung In was ahead on points which meant he would have won the fight. If the referee said it was an accidental punch, then the guy who did the punching won the fight. This means that Berna won the fight and became the champion. The crowd went wild. They said Sung In was ahead on the scorecard, so he should have won the fight. Several people connected with the event approached the commissioner while I sat at the table. They were ranting and raving expressing their displeasure with the decision. I had to remind them who they were talking to. I told them if they wanted to discuss the outcome they needed to calm down and speak in English so I could understand their complaints. They said that Berna should not have won the fight. I went in the ring to talk to Cortez, I asked him how he ruled on the punch. Was it intentional or accidental? Cortez said he called it a legal and fair punch, "I knew he couldn't continue so I called off the fight."

149

Berna won by TKO. They couldn't understand that Sung In was trying to strategize by saying he couldn't continue with the fight, thinking he would win on points. He couldn't win on points because the referee made the call-in opposition to what he thought it should have been. The people weren't happy and began to make threats. I left the ring and went to stand with my wife when I realized the Koreans wouldn't let Cortez out of the ring until he changed the decision. I told them that wasn't going to happen.

The Korean police referred to as the ROK (Republic of Korea) had to assist us in the arena with the unruly crowd. I told the ROK to get my referee out of the ring. Cortez said that he was scared because he wasn't sure what those people were planning to do to him. I told Cortez not to worry, we were being escorted back to the hotel. There were two guys, one from Japan and one from Korea who came to my hotel room trying to get me to change the decision. I told them it wasn't going to happen because Sung In legitimately lost the fight. I gave them the option to continue working with our federation or they could walk away. The Japanese tried to intercede but had to tell the Koreans that I wasn't going to change the decision. I contacted Berna's and Sung In's promoters and had them come to my room. I told them the fight was over and Berna won. All the squabbling needed to cease. My suggestion to each of them was to have a rematch between the two fighters within 180 days, either in the Philippines or Korea. The promoters reluctantly shook hands.

As we prepared to leave, I told Cortez to hurry up and get on the plane. I didn't want to push our luck. He laughed and said he was going to stay close to my wife and me because we had the ROK around us. We made it home safely and that became another memorable event during my time as the IBF President.

CHAPTER 80

The members of the IBF prided themselves on how thorough we trained our officials. We were known for recruiting the best to represent our organization and the sport of boxing. We held seminars in New Jersey and other cities around the country with the help of local promoters. One seminar took place in Norfolk, Virginia. Doug Beavers, our ratings chairman, arranged with a promoter to hold eighteen amateur boxing matches in one night. We invited judges and referees from around the world to attend. They were able to fly into Norfolk where we secured rooms at the Norfolk Holiday Inn. They were transported to the arena the next day to demonstrate their boxing skills.

Before the boxing matches, we had a seminar for the officials that Beavers managed. They used the expertise of Al Rothenberg and other judges to lay out the rules and regulations of boxing. We had a supervisor of officials named James Rondeau, he was the IBF's First Vice President. He would grade the officials by using scorecards and had a separate scorecard to grade the referees. We had a nice turnout with people coming from Australia, Korea, Japan, Lybia, Europe, and Hawaii to participate because they said it was an opportunity to gain knowledge. Most of the commissions paid for their officials to attend the event. It was their chance to become involved with the IBF as a world-class judge or referee.

To assess the participants, Rondeau would draw up plans for those who would be officiating each fight. He gave scorecards to the judges so they could offer their opinion on the officials' performances. Rondeau had a chance to look at every referee and he took into consideration the judges' scorecards. On the final day Rondeau, Beavers, Brennan, and I had a meeting to discuss the training sessions.

The reviews of the IBF seminars were positive, and we received several invitations to hold them in other places, such as California, Florida, Detroit, Morroco, Venezuela, and North Africa. Our seminars were successful, and I made sure to attend as many of them as I could. The participants asked a lot of questions and we gave them a lot of answers. We found that our officials were second to none, and they were even more qualified after attending our workshops. I had no qualms having them represent the IBF as I sent them around the world to officiate.

Jersey Joe mentioned that we had many African American fighters in the ring, but the people who judge ringside were always Caucasian. He said that something had to change, and it was up to us to change it. We started to recruit people who had been in the boxing business. We needed individuals who not only knew how to move around the ring but was familiar with the judging process. We utilized their services around New Jersey and as we formed the IBF, we used their services worldwide. When people called upon the IBF for officials for championship fights, I would let them know that I would be sending them either a judge or a referee of color; I didn't want them to think the IBF was another Latin American oriented organization officiated and controlled by Caucasians. The IBF was a worldwide federation that people came from around the world to box and officiate. That's what enabled us to grow. We extended an olive branch to all the countries that previously hadn't been invited to participate in the world of boxing. They were grateful to finally be included.

CHAPTER 81

After the fall of apartheid in the Union of South Africa, Nelson Mandela ran for and became the president of South Africa. The IBF had opened doors for Ncita to become a champion. We also made it possible for the South African fighter Vuyana Bungu to follow in Ncita's footsteps. Bungu was preparing to defend his title in Sun City, South Africa with promoters Cedric Kushner and Rodney Berman. They wanted to show Mr. Mandela how race relations had progressed. My wife and I were invited to attend the featured boxing match. We flew from JFK airport in New York to Johannesburg, South Africa, made the rounds with the press, and fulfilled our obligations as the head of the IBF.

The press was interested in the fact that the IBF had opened doors for South African boxers on a worldwide level. They wanted to know if we were going to approve future matches in South Africa. As someone always ready to promote boxing, I seized the opportunity to attend numerous upcoming matches in South Africa to support their fighters.

Mr. Berman notified my wife and me that once we left the press conference, we were to meet with Mr. Nelson Mandela. We flew from Johannesburg to Cape Town in a small plane that held about six people. When we arrived in Cape Town, we were introduced to Steven Tshwete who had been incarcerated with President Mandela on Robin Island for several years but was currently a member of his cabinet. He remained a close friend and confidant of the president.

We entered President Mandela's office and proceeded to talk about boxing while enjoying tea and cookies. Mr. Mandela questioned why there were so many sanctioning bodies in boxing. I explained that our emergence on the scene of boxing was in response to the needs of numerous young and upcoming athletes who weren't given a chance to fight for world titles.

I reminded the president that some of the representatives on our board as well as myself had been overlooked and unable to be successful in boxing because the doors had previously been closed to people of color. We all understood how difficult it could be, because we had all tasted that bitter pill of racism. Now that people of color were in control, we could open doors for others. That's exactly what we did. The president said that he appreciated our dedication to those who didn't have a voice.

We stepped out on his veranda outside of his office and took photos. The view of the ocean where the Indian Ocean met the Atlantic Ocean was magnificent and one that I wouldn't forget. Mr. Mandela bid us adieu and promised if he became available, he would be pleased to attend the upcoming fight to show his support for our federation and the boxers of South Africa.

I was grateful for what we were able to do in South Africa once apartheid ended, we had the respect of the officials in their country. We did the same in Australia. This was something the other federations hadn't been able to do. I knew that you couldn't call yourself a worldwide organization while living in a vacuum. I shared my private phone number with commissioners and promoters worldwide, they knew I was there if they needed me. This meant I sometimes received calls in the middle of the night, but I knew I had to be available if we were going to continue to grow.

President Nelson Mandela, Executive Secretary of South African Boxing Commission, and Bobby Lee

ROUND 15
"THE TRAITOR"

CHAPTER 82

"A Nation can survive its fools and even the ambitious. But it cannot survive treason from within. An enemy at the gates is less formidable, for he is known, and he carries his banners openly against the city.

But the traitor moves among those within the gates freely, his sly whispers rustling through all alleys, heard in the very halls of government itself.

for the traitor appears no traitor, he speaks in the accents familiar to his victim, and he wears their face and their garments, and he appeals to the baseness that lies deep in the hearts of all men.

He rots the soul of a nation; he works secretly and unknown in the night to undermine the pillars of the city: he infects the body politic so that it can no longer resist. A murderer is less to be feared. The traitor is the plague."__ Marcus Tullius Cicero

CHAPTER 83

On October 21, 1998, my nephew Darryl was taking me to the office and then to the airport for my flight to Virginia for my meeting with Bill Brennan and Doug Beavers. On the way to the office we picked up my daughter and took her to Beth Israel Hospital. She'd had bunion surgery and was walking with crutches. Her doctor, Alice Cohen, who treated her Sickle Cell wanted Cheryl to stop in so she could examine her to make sure she was healing properly. We picked her up and waited for her to get situated in the back seat. I explained to her that I was going to Virginia for business and she needed to call Darryl when she was ready to leave the hospital. We dropped her off on the lower level of the hospital close to Cohen's office. I kissed and hugged her and told her to call her mother or her brother if she had any problems. I assured her that they would come right away. I kissed her cheek again and told her that I would see her when I returned.

Darryl and I drove to the office in East Orange. I called Beavers in Virginia and told him that I was about to leave New Jersey and my flight would arrive in Norfolk around one o'clock. He was to pick me up at the airport and then we would meet with Brennan. What I didn't know at the time was Beavers was wearing a wire when we were speaking on the phone. He was still wearing it when he picked me up from the airport.

When we spoke on the phone, I asked Beavers about the money that he owed me. I lent him 15,000 dollars seven months earlier to keep him from losing his home. He signed a promissory note stating the amount he owed me to protect my interest. He had a balance of 11,000 dollars and I told him he could pay me back when he was able. Beavers said that he would have some cash for me when I got to Virginia. I didn't mind giving money out of my pocket for a person who I thought was not only a business partner but also a friend.

When I arrived in Virginia, Beavers was waiting for me at the airport. Brennan, Beavers, and I normally met in Virginia because they both lived there. That meant one airline ticket and one hotel room. We would meet quarterly and once we finished our business, we would get something to eat. Brennan would then make the hour long drive home. Beavers would take me to the airport and make the thirty-minute trip home. On the way to the hotel, we discussed the IBF and boxing news.

When we arrived at the Holiday Inn in Norfolk and approached the front desk I asked if they had a room for Robert W. Lee. Beavers interrupted saying he had the room registered in his name. I thought that was unusual and asked him what made him decide to do that. He said they didn't have any suites available where you could sleep and have a meeting, so I got two rooms, one where we could work and one where you could sleep. He said they were next door to each other.

As the clerk prepared my paperwork, he mentioned to Beavers that the other guys that he was waiting on were already there. I asked Doug if he knew who the clerk was referring to. He said he didn't know of anyone else besides Brennan that would be meeting with us. I told Beavers that the clerk probably had him mixed up with someone else. Beavers asked the clerk if Brennan had checked in. The clerk said he was supposed to tell us that Brennan was grabbing a bite to eat in the lunchroom, and we were to join him. After a while, Brennan said he wanted to start the meeting so that he could make it home before it got dark.

When we got to the room Beavers handed me the key to my room. I entered, set my bags on the bed, and went into the room that Beavers reserved for our meeting. We began the meeting by discussing the placement of fighters and out of nowhere Beavers pulled out a couple of envelopes from his sock and handed them to Brennan and me. I asked him what the envelopes were for and he said it was a little present for us. I asked him why he was walking around the streets of Norfolk with money in his socks. He said there were bad people in the area, and he didn't want any trouble.

We continued to discuss business until I excused myself to go to the men's room. I went into my hotel room to use the facilities and contemplated taking my insulin. I decided that I would take it later. I removed my jacket and left it in my room because it was getting warm in the other room. We resumed our meeting upon my return. We talked about promoters and how we planned to schedule our upcoming bouts. If there was any kind of disagreement on how the fighter should be rated, we left it up to Beavers to decide. He was good at his job, one of the best in the world. Beavers would spend his evenings in front of multiple televisions that we purchased for him, watching the cable paid for by the IBF. He not only watched fights from the United States, but he also watched fights from other countries. Beavers was knowledgeable on the fighters and their capabilities in the ring.

After meeting for a couple of hours and scheduling my next visit, Brennan left before it got dark. Beavers and I continued talking after Brennan left. He gave a breakdown on various fighters, giving me the reason for each of their ratings. I accepted his explanations because that was his area of expertise. Around 6 pm Beavers said he was going home to have dinner. I reminded him that my flight left at seven and he should arrive around six so that I could make it to the airport on time. I walked Beavers to the elevator and told him to tell his family hello. I went back to the meeting room, propped my feet up, and enjoyed watching the news.

About fifteen minutes after Beavers left there was a knock on the door. When I looked through the peephole there were two men and a woman standing on the other side. When I opened the door, they introduced themselves. The first man was Agent Richards and the woman was Agent Riley both from the FBI. The other man was a representative of the Department of Treasury. Agent Richards explained that the room was registered under the FBI and had been under surveillance for several hours. He said they had taken pictures and recorded everything that transpired in the room. I told them that was good, and I hope they enjoyed themselves.

Richards said that the FBI had an ongoing investigation of Don King and they needed help to bring him to justice. I asked him what that had to do with me. Richards said they wanted me to give them information on cash that may have been paid to me by King. I told them I received a very nice salary from the IBF, and I have since I joined the organization. I asked them if they wanted to see every penny that I made, or I could show them my W-2's. I suggested they ask the IRS how much I made through the years. Riley asked me about any illegal transactions that occurred between King and me. I told her that she was talking to the wrong guy because King and I had no reason to have transactions between the two of us.

King is a promoter who deals with the managers and promoters of the fighters. They make their deals amongst each other and initiate the contracts needed to fight. Once they have that in order, they deliver them to us and ask our permission to promote the fight. No money passes between promoters and the sanctioning bodies The IBF is a sanctioning body.

Once the fight is approved by the IBF the promoter must pay a sanction fee to put the fight on. The fighter pays a sanctioning fee for the right to fight for the title. When they pay it is usually in the form of a check. This is the only time money exchanges hands. Richards accused King of giving me and the IBF money to put on fights and to place fighters in the ratings who didn't belong. I said I'm not the greatest chairman but I'm pretty much aware of what goes on in the rating system. All that I could tell them is that no money changed hands between Don King and I. Even if it had, I'm not a rat. There was no way that I, as an African American man, would turn against another African American man for some trumped-up charges just because you are intimidated by his success.

I told them that they should use the cadre' of FBI agents and officers to whom they are paying a sizeable salary. I shouldn't be doing their job. I told them just how they approached me to ask questions, they could do the same with Don King. Riley said that wasn't what they were looking for. I said that I gathered that, you want me to be a snitch, but you're barking up the wrong tree. I told them I wasn't going to help them take down a Black man, I knew how they operated. They searched for African Americans who have obtained some notoriety for the success they have obtained, and the money they've made and try to bring them down. They informed me that they could make life miserable for me if I didn't cooperate. I told them that I knew they could make life miserable for anyone who didn't have any brains in their heads, but I wasn't going to roll over and let them step on me or anyone else. I told them it was up to them to accept what I was saying to them, but I wasn't going to be a pawn in their little game.

CHAPTER 84

Next, they called in two assistant US attorneys. One was Jose Sierra and the other was Marc Agniflo. They introduced them to me, and I tried to explain the conversation that had transpired before them coming in. They asked the FBI agents what my response was. They told them that I said I hadn't done anything illegal with Don King or anyone else. I began to realize that Beavers was behind this someway somehow. He had to have mentioned something about the ratings for these people to broach the subject on people being paid to alter the ratings. What I later discovered is they came to Beavers and told him they wanted to talk to him about the IBF and Beavers was rumored to have said: "What took you so long?" As I sat Beavers down and told him they were going after Don King. He said that he didn't know anything about Don King. I'm not sure what he knew but they gave him full immunity from prosecution, he would eventually tell them everything they wanted to know.

Sierra was the lead attorney, said he was going to be honest with me. He said if I didn't help them, they were going to come after me. He said they would arrest me, indict me, take me to trial, and destroy the IBF as it's known. I told them to take their best shot because if they thought I was going to fold over and beg for mercy they were wrong. The phone in the room began to ring and Richards answered it. I asked if the phone was for me, but I was ignored. He told whoever was on the other end that I was in a meeting and I would get back to them as soon as the meeting was over. When he hung up the phone, I asked him who was on the phone. Richards said it was my wife, I asked him why he didn't give me the phone. I explained that my daughter was in the hospital and I needed to know if everything was alright. Richards said he didn't give me the phone because we were in a meeting. I told him my family was more important than this meeting, and I didn't appreciate him screening my phone calls.

The interrogation continued and Richards mentioned the thousand dollars that Beavers had given me in the envelope. He said the FBI gave Beavers the money to give to me. I explained that Beavers owed me 11,000 dollars and he told me that he was giving me 1,000 dollars toward the balance of the loan. I told Richards the money was from a personal loan and had nothing to do with boxing. Sierra stated that they had given Beavers marked bills to give to me as bribe money. I knew at that moment they were trying to set me up and my so-called friend, Doug Beavers, had turned on me.

At that moment I realized that I hadn't taken my insulin and told them I needed to go next door to my room to take my insulin shot. They sent Richards and the IRS agent with me. When I got to the room and opened the door, Richards pushed me into the room. I had my jacket hanging on a hanger and Richards grabbed it. I asked him what he thought he was doing with my jacket, and he said he wanted to check it. I reminded him that he didn't have a warrant to check my clothing or anything else in my room. He said he was checking it anyway. He removed the envelope that I received from Beavers and said he was going to keep it because the money belonged to them. I didn't argue. I took my insulin shot and we all returned to the other room.

Richards told Sierra that he had the envelope with the money that they had given to Beavers, the money I supposedly accepted as a bribe. Sierra said if I cooperated with them, they would make the bribery charge go away. I reminded them that I wasn't having anything to do with their little set-up, and I couldn't tell them what I didn't know. I had never taken money from King for anything. I didn't have that type of association with him. Sierra said he knew King and I were close. I told him we've had our ups and downs, but we are in the same business, so we work together for the good of our organizations. Sierra said they were coming after me if I didn't help them and they were going to use the transaction between Doc (their nickname for Beavers) and me to show that I accepted a bribe from him. I told them I hoped that they were going to give me my money back because it was a payment towards Beavers' outstanding balance. They finally decided that they were finished with the interrogation and proceeded to leave, telling me that I could go back to whatever it was that I was doing. I returned to my room because I didn't know how many cameras and listening devices, they had hidden in the meeting room.

CHAPTER 85

I immediately called my wife when I got back into my room. I explained to her how some guys had me tied up in a meeting and wouldn't let me answer the phone. My wife told me that I needed to get in touch with my son or Grace (my children's mother) because Cheryl had taken a turn for the worse. I tried unsuccessfully to reach my son, so I called Al Lucas who worked with me and told him that I was trying to reach my son or his mother. I asked if he had seen either of them. Al said no, but I needed to be strong. I asked him why he was saying that I needed to be strong. Al asked me if I knew that Cheryl had passed. I said that I didn't know anything about my daughter passing. I couldn't believe my ears. It still grieves me to talk about the loss of my one and only daughter. I couldn't understand how my daughter died when all she did was go in to have her foot checked to make sure it was healing properly. I finally reached Grace and asked what was going on. Grace said it was true, that our daughter had passed. She said that she had spent the last four hours at the hospital. I told Grace that I was confused because when we dropped her off at the hospital she was tipping on her crutches and feeling good.

Grace said they called my office to tell me Cheryl had taken a turn for the worse, which I didn't understand because she only went in for a check-up. Grace said they ended up having to give her transfusions and the blood was going in and coming right back out. Her organs began to shut down. I couldn't believe this all came about from foot surgery. I believed they had done something to cause her stress. Grace said Cheryl was in the morgue at the hospital and she and Robert were on their way home. I asked her to put my son on the phone so I could get his version of what happened.

Robert Jr. tearfully said they had done everything that they could, but they couldn't save her. He explained that they gave her morphine which was against Grace's wishes because she knew morphine would only mask any problems that Cheryl may have had. I told Robert Jr. that I wouldn't be able to make it home until morning. They wanted me to come sooner, but I told them because of the flights, tomorrow morning would be the earliest that I could get home. I told them that I would arrive around 8:30 a.m. Robert Jr. said he would be there to pick me up.

I went to the front desk to get another room because I didn't like the way things were going. I asked the guy at the front desk what he meant earlier about the other guys who were already there. He apologized and said that he couldn't answer my question. I told him that he did know something. The clerk apologized again and said he was just an employee and he wasn't allowed to say anything else. I knew that he was aware of the actions of the FBI, and he had been threatened to keep his mouth shut. I told him that I wasn't happy with the way things went down and I wanted to move to a different room that was free of bugs and cameras. He gave me another room. I tried to get some sleep so that I could mentally prepare to see my beloved daughter the next day.

The next morning, I called a taxi to take me to the airport, I didn't want to be bothered with Beavers the traitor. While sitting on the plane the two FBI agents walked past me. I had a few choice names that I called them under my breath. When I got home my son was waiting for me and took me first to see my wife and then to the hospital. I wanted to talk to the doctor to find out exactly what happened. I couldn't locate Dr. Cohen so I spoke with another doctor who said they would let me see Cheryl after they cleaned her up. I stood next to my beautiful daughter and talked to her even though I knew that I would never hear her sweet voice again. I cried a river of tears while my son and Grace waited in the hallway. Finally, my son entered the room and told me that it was time to leave. I hated to leave because I knew this was one of the last times that I would see her.

On the way home, we stopped at a restaurant for a bite to eat and then they dropped me off at my home. The time had come to make the arrangements for Cheryl's services. We knew a mortician in Westfield at a funeral home called Clinton-Curry. They gave us an estimate on funeral expenses, and when they showed me the price tag for their services I nearly jumped out of my chair. One of the saving graces was when they were in elementary school, the board of education arranged for students to receive an insurance policy. It cost around sixty dollars per child a year. It was a five-thousand-dollar policy. I took advantage of an offer to increase the policy by another five thousand for an additional fee increasing the value to ten thousand dollars. I told Grace that I would go to the insurance office after I received the death certificates to file the claim. I paid for everything upfront and thankfully we didn't have any issues with the insurance company with paying the death benefits.

Cheryl's services were held at St. Johns Baptist Church located in Scotch Plains where we were all members. We had the viewing the night before her funeral. Cheryl's funeral was one of the largest that I ever attended. With her being young and knowing so many young people, they came in droves to pay their final respects. The turnout was amazing. One of our cousins spoke during the funeral along with a few friends and community leaders. It was an exceptional homegoing celebration.

CHAPTER 86

That time in my life took a lot out of me. It was a double whammy. I had the incident in Virginia with the feds, I learned a loyal friend was a traitor, and to top it off I lost my beautiful daughter. The final straw was when two sportswriters, one from the New York Post and the other from the New York Daily News wrote an article saying that Don King had paid for my daughter's funeral. I protested saying the story was a lie. I explained that I'd had the policy since Cheryl was in elementary school. In fact, it was the only policy that I was able to get for her due to her pre-existing condition of Sickle Cell Anemia. I told them that King never paid for anything, I paid for everything for my baby girl. They were making a bad situation worse.

I called Don King to ask him why he would say that he paid for Cheryl's funeral when he knew that wasn't true. King said that he was trying to help. I told him if he wanted to help; send flowers. That incident drove a wedge between the two of us for several years. From that day forward I knew that I would never be a complete man because a piece of my heart left with my daughter. I couldn't sleep and I lost my appetite. My pastor and several deacons from St. Johns Baptist Church came to my house to console me. I was inconsolable. I was so down that I had to reach up to tie my shoes.

CHAPTER 87

When I got back to the office, I had a pile of work waiting for me. I would go in early and stay late, but I had a hard time concentrating on what needed to be done. I planned to retire in the year 2000, but I realized that I wasn't going to make it that long. I asked my colleagues if Beavers had called. They said they hadn't heard from him. I knew that what he had done to me in Virginia is something that I would never forget. I started getting my business in order as I prepared to step down as the IBF president. I put my attorney on notice telling him that I may need his services soon. Linda Torres, who previously helped with some legal work contacted me. She'd been notified that the FBI had conducted a sting operation on me in Virginia. She called my legal counsel Walter Stone to ask him if he had heard about it. Stone said he hadn't. He called me and I told him that what he had heard was true, they had gotten to me and I wasn't sure what to do next.

Stone told me the first thing that I needed to do was to hire a good criminal attorney and give him the information that I had access to because the IBF would be subpoenaed. He said they were probably going to try and jam me up since I wouldn't cooperate with their demands. Torres recommended a couple of attorneys that she thought would represent me. I decided to go with Gerald Krovatin out of Chatham, New Jersey. I called Krovatin and introduced myself and told him that I was interested in retaining his services. He set up a meeting for the following Monday.

I explained to Krovatin the details of what happened in Virginia and how I was totally blindsided by their accusations. Krovatin told me to prepare for them to subpoena my records and he told me to start copying my paperwork. He also wanted me to give him a copy of everything that the feds requested from our organization. Krovatin said his retainer would be 20,000 dollars and he would notify the FBI that he would be representing me.

A few weeks later they sent Krovatin paperwork saying they wanted to file what's called a Bill Of. They wanted me to complete the document using my records. I worked on the document and when it was complete, I took it to my attorney, and he sent it to the FBI. Krovatin suggested that I take a leave of absence from the IBF to focus on the case. I sent a letter to the board saying that I would be stepping down as the IBF's president until we were able to resolve the situation.

My executive secretary, Marian Muhammad, who I appointed to the position at the IBF, had a smug look on her face when I told everyone in the office what Beavers had done in Virginia. I didn't understand at the time why she had an odd expression on her face, but later I discovered the reason. She was sneaking around behind my back and giving the FBI information on the organization. I was given this information by Agent Richards. Richards said Marian wanted to become IBF's next president. She helped the FBI to get me out of the way. I told him, "It looks like she succeeded."

I appointed Hiawatha Knight, who lived in Detroit, Michigan as acting president during my leave. She had been a loyal member of our organization. Marian and some of our members treated Knight badly and they didn't respect her. Indeed, she wasn't as well versed in the business as I was, but that was no excuse for them to treat her the way they did. She would fly from Detroit to Newark and when she would ask members to join her for dinner, they would ignore her requests. Eventually, she'd had enough of the disrespect, so she resigned and passed the presidency to Marian Muhammad. That's what Muhammad was hoping to gain, and that's exactly what she got. My son couldn't take over because we both had to vacate the office. Little did we know the FBI had my son on their radar too.

CHAPTER 88

My son was my right-hand man and I had planned to pass the reins of the IBF presidency to him after my retirement. Unfortunately, the feds had different plans for the two of us. My son and I were both indicted on the same day. There was a 200,000-dollar bond for my son and a 200,000-dollar bond for me. Grace, my former wife, used her house as collateral for Robert Jr., and I used my house to cover my bond. We were fortunate that we didn't have to spend the night in jail knowing the possibility of harassment by the police due to the color of our skin. As the president of the USBA-I, I wasn't considered a threat, but it appeared that once I became president of the IBF all hell broke loose.

The FBI wanted to put their feet on the necks of African Americans to stop us from progressing. Other nationalities are permitted to come to America and set up shop and create successful businesses. Many times, in Black neighborhoods. African Americans aren't afforded all the grants and tax breaks simply because of how we came to America. When African Americans apply to the Small Business Association for money, their entire ancestry is investigated, and they are still denied the loan. It was apparent that the FBI was going to ensure that a Black man with all the attention and power that I had acquired would be silenced. One way or another.

CHAPTER 89

It still disturbs me that I didn't recognize that there was a traitor within our ranks. I was taught a long time ago to be mindful of those in your circle. As I found out, a person that I considered a friend had their hands in everyone's pockets. Doug Beavers, our ratings chairman, asked for immunity from prosecution by the United States Attorneys Jose Sierra and Marc Agniflo. I lost respect for the FBI after their so-called investigation on my son and I. Beavers told the FBI that he would tell them everything he knew. The FBI was known for putting the squeeze on one person to get to another. Unfortunately, I thought Beavers and I were on the same page.

I didn't pay attention to the little things that were happening. I ended up trying to outrun things that were being thrown at me from the left and the right. There were too many obstacles in my path. Beavers and a few others fabricated so many stories that if they had noses like Pinocchio they would have stretched from Jersey to Juniper. It's a fact that a White man can tell a lie, and everyone believes it, but a Black man tells the truth and it's questionable.

Late summer in the year 2000, my son and I both went to trial in the federal courthouse in Newark, New Jersey. My son was charged with five counts and I was charged with thirty-three counts, twenty-eight of them were for RICO (Racketeer Influenced and Corrupt Organizations) violations. The remaining five charges were for interstate travel, racketeering, and one charge for income tax evasion. The jury selection began, and it took a couple of days because it was such a big case. They had challenges finding people for the jury because of the expected length of the trial. During the discovery proceeding, we received word that the prosecutor, Jose Sierra, was going to enter the illegal search of my clothing into evidence.

The Friday before the trial started, Krovatin sent a request to the judge asking that he not permit testimony related to the actions of the FBI against me in Virginia. He asked that the judge strike the evidence from the case because they made an illegal search of my jacket. Krovatin said that evidence should not be allowed. The judge alerted the prosecution about Krovatin's request. The judge said he was considering siding with the defense on the matter because the search did not appear to be legal. Sierra jumped up and told the judge that he couldn't do that. The judge told Sierra they had ample time to get a search warrant, so the evidence they obtained wasn't admissible. Sierra told the judge that he was taking away the strongest part of their case. He said without that evidence they didn't have a case. The judge told them they should have done their job, and unless they convinced him by Monday that the search was legal, the evidence would be thrown out. My attorney was pleased and told me that we had gotten a break. We had said all along that they conducted an illegal search by reaching into my jacket and removing my money.

Monday morning, we entered the courtroom expecting the judge to deliver the decision that was discussed on Friday. Krovatin pointed out a woman in the courtroom who he said was one of the rising stars to the US attorney as an appellate litigator. He said she was there to make sure things go right for the government. Her job was to make sure the judge doesn't dismiss the illegal search because that will ruin the government's case. The judge called my attorney, Robert Jr's attorney, the law assistant, and the two US attorneys into his chambers. I was feeling confident at that moment that justice would be served.

They must have stayed in the judge's chambers for nearly forty-five minutes, and when they emerged Krovatin's face was long. He said the judge was going to allow the evidence from the search. I couldn't believe my ears. I reminded Krovatin what the judge said on Friday. Krovatin said who knows what has happened since Friday, but he said if we had a complaint, we had the right to file an appeal. I said even Ray Charles could see this wasn't right, I wasn't stupid. I knew that over the weekend someone had reached out and touched the judge and warned him not to throw out the evidence.

CHAPTER 90

Krovatin planned to draft the appeal papers immediately so when the trial was over, we could file a brief with the appellate division. If I was convicted, we would ask that the decision be overturned and request a new trial. It became apparent that I was battling the prosecutors, both US attorneys, two federal agents, the treasury, and the judge. His actions were blatant, and he didn't seem to care who knew it. As the trial began and the FBI agents took the stand, they seemed to set the tone for the trial. As I sit there with my fate in the hands of "the people", I reflected on the events that transpired on that fateful day in Virginia.

Beavers took the stand and every question asked of him seemed to focus on the "bribe" money. He repeated bribe money over and over like a forty-five record with a scratch. Beavers dealt with numerous managers, trainers, and promoters. If anyone was able to shake somebody down, it was him. Most of my deals were by telephone or in writing. They tried to say that King gave me money to have the fighters rated. Beavers would rate these guys, then send me the information so that I could review it. We would then share the data with our members and our media specialists.

Being a ratings chairman requires numerous hours of assessing fighters, monitoring records, and creating reports. Beavers lived in Norfolk, Virginia, so fight results wouldn't reach him immediately. With me being right across from New York, the media center of the world, I would receive the information promptly and then share it with Beavers so that he could update the ratings. There would be times when he would send me the ratings before a fight took place. I would have to make changes to reflect the winners and losers. I wasn't going to send erroneous ratings out because as the CEO of the IBF the buck stopped with me. That's why I checked the ratings, letters, and other materials that passed through my office because I was in charge and I wanted to protect the IBF's reputation.

Beavers was asked if he was claiming that I had changed the ratings and added an undeserving fighter to the lineup without his knowledge. Beavers said that sometimes we communicated and sometimes we didn't, but he didn't always know the results of the ratings until they were sent back to him. Beavers identified several fighters and their promoters. Then they asked him if any of the promoters paid me to get their fighters rated. He claimed if they had it was considered a bribe. I couldn't believe how my "friend" had turned on me. He was sinking my ship pretty good. Here we were again when a White man says something against a Black man, we know which one will be believed. This is especially true in the courtroom. It amazed me how they were believing everything he was saying. Then he began to go overboard with his accusations. It was obvious that he was trying to jam me up.

US Attorney: Mr. Beavers, did you have meetings with the promoters of the boxing matches?

Doug Beavers: Yes.

US Attorney: Did you ever meet with Cedric Kushner?

Doug Beavers: Yes.

US Attorney: Did you receive 100,000 dollars from Cedric Kushner?

Doug Beavers: Yes, I did.

US Attorney: What were you supposed to do with the 100,000 dollars?

Doug Beavers: Split it four ways between Mr. Robert Lee Sr., Mr. Robert Lee Jr., Mr. Bill Brennan and me.

US Attorney: (Walking away) I have no further questions, your honor.

I must mention that on the jury of my peers there were three Black people. Beavers stayed on the witness stand for a couple of days. Finally, it was time for my attorney to cross-examine the traitor.

Krovatin: Mr. Beavers, are you a liar?

Doug Beavers: Well, I don't know. Why?

Krovatin: Mr. Beavers, you said some promoters wanted to organize some fights, but you needed approval from Mr. Lee. You said they were from West Virginia. Was that the truth?

Doug Beavers: No, that was a lie.

My attorney grilled Beavers who admitted that at least four of his statements were lies. Krovatin asked Beavers about the rest of his testimony and shot each lie down one by one. I got annoyed listening to his trail of lies. The frustrating part is that you can't say anything, you must listen as someone intentionally tries to destroy your life.

During a break, Krovatin asked me where Beavers was getting all the stories from that he was telling on the stand. I told him that I had no idea because his stories had no validity. I told him if anybody met with the promoters and lined their pockets with greenbacks, it was Beavers. I knew he admitted to meeting with promoters and getting money on the side because he was promised immunity from the Feds. Beavers claimed the money was given to him, but it was supposed to be delivered to me. I never saw or heard about the money that Beavers referred to. Other than being a heavy drinker and smoking like a chimney, I don't know what Beavers may have done with the money he was siphoning from our clients. I know it wasn't coming or going in my wallet. This is a case of "selective racial prosecution".

CHAPTER 91

Bob Arum, the president of Top Rank, was next to testify. Arum had been one of the IBF's strongest supporters since our inception. He was the one who sent Marvin Hagler our way which put the IBF on the map in 1983. He helped us with fights in and around the country. Arum had a way of antagonizing people, that's what he did with the WBC and WBA. They didn't like working with him. We were happy to promote Arum's fighters because of all the support he gave our organization.

When Arum testified, they asked him about a situation involving George Foreman when he fought for the IBF's heavyweight title. Michael Moorer was the heavyweight champion in 1994 and George Foreman wanted to fight for the title. Everyone knew Foreman was past his prime, but he was a big man with a big name, and he had a serious punch. Foreman went to Arum to have him promote the fight. Arum agreed to promote the fight along with Lou Duva because Duva was promoting Moorer at the time.

The fight was set for November 5, 1994, at the MGM Grand Las Vegas. The fight was billed as "One for the Ages". Moorer took the fight to Foreman and was ahead on the scorecards. The fight started to turn around in the tenth round when Foreman's punches seemed to be affecting Moorer. Before the end of the round, a punch stunned Moorer and he fell to the canvas and received a ten-count from referee Joe Cortez. George became the oldest fighter, only a little over two months from his forty-sixth birthday to win the heavyweight champion of the world. The record had been held by Jersey Joe Walcott.

When you come in as a champion, you must make a mandatory defense against the leading contender within nine months. The leading contender was a fighter by the name of Francois Botha, a White South

African. George knew that he was obligated to fight Botha within those nine months. What customarily happens is the fighters usually take a hiatus between the time the champion wins and the time he gets ready to fight the mandatory. In between, he's able to fight someone else in the ratings to make money. He then fights the mandatory. If he loses the title, he's at least had the opportunity to make some money. Arum called me to say that George knew he had to fight the mandatory, but he wanted an optional fight against a guy from Germany named Axel Schulz because he couldn't find anyone else in the ratings who was going to have the marquee value to give him a good payday. Cedric Kushner approached me and said that Schulz had agreed to fight Foreman.

April 22, 1995 was the scheduled date of the Foreman-Schulz bout at the MGM Grand in Las Vegas. No one thought Foreman would have any problems with Schulz after coming off with a big win over Moorer making him the toast of the town. Everybody wanted to see Foreman win. Axel Schulz danced around a slow and sluggish Foreman. The fight ended with a majority decision. Two judges went for Foreman and one for Schulz. The crowd booed because they believed that Schulz had won the fight. George knew that he got away by the skin of his teeth. I didn't think that Axel did enough to defeat George, but he handled himself well. When the fight was over, the crowd became rowdy and began throwing things and yelling at the judges. Arum and I were discussing the match and when I told him my feelings about Schulz's performance, we concluded that there should be a rematch. Arum was pleased because each fighter stood to have a decent payday. Around that time Kushner and Wilfrid Sauerland arrived ringside to where Arum and I were standing. Kushner said, "Bob that was a tough one, but I didn't think George won that fight." I said that might be your thoughts, but we must abide by the judges' decision, and the judges say that Foreman retained his title. We told them we decided to have a rematch to satisfy disappointed fans. They both agreed that it was a good idea. I asked Wilfrid and Arum if they would promote the fight. I said that I would contact Bill Brennan and let him know that we're going to schedule a rematch within 180 days. Any longer and we would be jeopardizing Botha's chance at the title.

When I called Brennan, he remarked on the closeness of the fight. He said that he didn't think Foreman won, but he didn't think that Schulz lost either. He said he thought that George performed well, but not as well as he should have. He said if he had there wouldn't be controversy surrounding the decision.

Our annual convention was usually held around Memorial Day weekend. In 1995 our convention was held in Atlanta, Georgia, at the Westin Peachtree Hotel. George Foreman, Axel Schulz, Evander Holyfield (he lives in Atlanta), Bob Arum, Cedric Kushner, and Wilfried Sauerland were in attendance. They were all talking about the Foreman- Schulz rematch. We were under the impression that Foreman was ready for the fight, which was scheduled to take place in the fall. Of course, things never run as smooth as you would like them to. After the convention was over, Arum returned to Las Vegas. A friend of Arum's named Stan Hoffman was visiting New York promoting the Houston Boxing Association. He said Arum was planning a trip to New York and wanted to know if he could meet with the two of us for lunch. I told Hoffman that I would take the train and meet them in NYC. Stan asked me to meet him at the Mayfair Hotel in Manhattan, and then we could meet up with Arum. When I arrived, Hoffman was standing outside waiting for me. He said there's a slight change of plans. He said we were going to talk to Arum before going to lunch. I asked Hoffman if he knew why Arum was calling this meeting. Hoffman said he believed it had something to do with George Foreman. I told Hoffman that I hoped George was busy preparing for the fight. We didn't want a repeat of the last match.

It was just the three of us in the room and Arum said he had something that he needed to discuss. He said that Foreman did not want a rematch with Axel Schulz. I said we all agreed that there would be a rematch. I asked Arum why Foreman was refusing to fight. Arum said that he knew he was supposed to deliver Foreman since he was his promoter, but Foreman wasn't happy with the purse. We were paying George 7.5 million and Schulz 2.5 million, but George was complaining that we were paying Schulz too much money to fight. I asked Arum why Foreman worried about how much Schulz would receive if he was pleased with what he is getting. I asked Arum who did Foreman want to fight. He said that he didn't know what was going through Foreman's head.

I told Arum that we had already mandated the fight and we've put it out to the media that this fight would take place in 180 days, and that's what we must stick with. Arum said he would try to convince him, but he said Foreman is insisting that he doesn't want to fight Schulz. I asked Arum if Foreman was afraid that he couldn't beat Schulz. Arum said he didn't know what Foreman was afraid of.

Axel Schultz, George Foreman, and Robert W. Lee Sr. 1995 IBF Convention Atlanta, Georgia

CHAPTER 92

After lunch, I took the train back to Jersey and when I arrived at the office, I called Brennan and told him that I was sick about the Foreman-Schulz situation. We had this fight set up and ready to go and Foreman goes and throws a monkey wrench into the situation. Brennan said that we couldn't back out now because we have announced the rematch and we already called for a purse bid. When you call for a purse bid the promoters have the right to make a sealed bid. The one with the highest bid earns the right to promote the fight. With a purse bid, the champion gets 75% and the challenger 25%, and that's what we would mandate. We called for the purse bid but Foreman said he wasn't going to fight. I explained to Arum if George refuses to fight, he would have to vacate his heavyweight championship title. I told Arum that it was up to George if he thought it was better to lose the title or to walk away from it.

Arum decided to reach out to Ron Withers, a friend of Foreman to see if he could talk some sense into him. I believe Foreman was concerned about losing his title to Schulz because he was adamant about not fighting. As the championship chairman Brennan vacated George Foreman's title because the purse bid was called, and Foreman refused to answer.

With Foreman out, we had to identify the highest two ranked fighters and allow them to fight for the heavyweight title. Francois Botha was ranked number one, and because Axel Schulz had been promised the opportunity to fight, he was rated number two. The ticket would be Botha-Schulz fighting for the heavyweight title. The fight was scheduled to take place in Germany on December 9, 1995. Although the Foreman-Schulz fight ended in controversy, Botha was declared the current heavyweight champion.

George Foreman went on to make millions selling the Foreman Grill worldwide. Botha was later disqualified because he tested positive for steroids after the fight and was fined 50,000 dollars by the IBF.

CHAPTER 93

During Arum's testimony, he stated that once I left him and Stanley at the Mayfair Hotel, Stanley told him that for the IBF to approve the fight between Foreman and Schulz he had to pay me 200,000 dollars. He said the money needed to be paid before the purse bid was called. Arum told Stanley that 200,000 dollars was too much money, but he would agree to pay 100,000 dollars. Stanley took the money using me as a scapegoat even though I knew nothing of this conversation or the request for money until Arum's testimony.

According to Arum, he gave the check to Stanley to give it to me. The only reason this information came to light is that during the screening of potential witnesses, the FBI subpoenaed Hoffman's financial records. When the FBI scoured Stanley's bank account the 100,000-dollar check that was supposedly given to me was still in Hoffman's bank account in Ellenville, New York. If Hoffman had never been subpoenaed, Arum would have gone to his grave thinking that I had hustled him out of 100,000 dollars.

Krovatin asked Arum if he believed Stanley gave me the check. Arum dropped his head and said that he didn't believe Hoffman gave me the money. Arum confessed that until the FBI disclosed the location of the check, he had no idea that Hoffman kept the money.

After Arum finished with his testimony Judge Bissell called a recess and everyone began to exit the courtroom. You should have seen Arum and Hoffman in the hallway. Arum was all over him like a cheap suit, yelling and shaking his fist in Hoffman's face. I thought Arum was going to punch him. I couldn't help but chuckle as I realized I was watching one White man scam another White man with my Black face in the middle.

I don't know if Arum ever got his money back, but I thought...here they were digging a hole for me and little did they know they would fall into it.

Arum continued with his testimony after the recess. He was asked if I had ever given him anything. He said no. Arum described how his company worked closely with our federation to put on several fights, and there were many times he worked at the IBF's conventions. Arum told Krovatin that I never asked him for money and I never gave him any. I was pleased to hear somebody finally telling the truth. I figured after they pulled the covers off Hoffman, he had to tell the truth.

The next person to testify was Cedric Kushner, originally from South Africa, he was in the entertainment business promoting rock concerts. Kushner ran into difficulties, something to do with ticketing and was barred from promoting concerts. He decided to go into the boxing industry and used his contacts in South Africa and Europe to corral several fighters. He planned to bring them to the United States to further their careers.

Kushner became friendly with Doug Beavers, and according to Beavers, they chatted two to three times per week to discuss Kushner's fighters and their placement in the ratings. This wasn't unusual. It was customary for managers to contact the ratings chairman of the sanctioning bodies to see if they could have their fighters elevated so they could fight for a title. Kushner, questioned by the US attorney, told them he had never given me any money, nor had I solicited money from him for favors for the IBF. He did state that when he needed help with ratings he would contact either Beavers, Brennan, or me. This was to get his fighters into meaningful bouts.

Cedric Kushner was the American representative for some of the boxers in Europe; namely Axel Schulz. Kushner testified that Beavers told him for the fight to be sanctioned by the IBF he would have to pay 100,000 dollars. Kushner said that he agreed to the fee, and he received the money from Sauerland. Kushner said Beavers drove to Long Island to pick up the funds and he claimed he was going to split the money among himself, Brennan, Robert Jr., and me. Needless to say, not only didn't we know about this transaction, but we never saw any of the money. We would have never known about this deception had it not been for the trial.

Kushner, when asked directly by the prosecutor and then by my attorney if he had ever given me any money responded that he had never given me money. He also stated that I had never asked him for money. He said Beavers came up with that idea. Under direct examination, Beavers stated that Kushner gave him the money that was supposedly split between the four of us. At this point the people in the courtroom, the jury included, were probably looking at Beavers like Geppetto looked at Pinocchio. Krovatin only kept Kushner on the stand long enough to prove that Brennan, Robert Jr., and I never asked for or received money from him.

CHAPTER 94

Following Kushner's testimony, it was boxing promoter Stanley Hoffman's turn to take the stand. Hoffman was a record producer for Savoy Records which operated out of Elizabeth, New Jersey. During the early '80s, Jersey Joe granted Hoffman a promoter's license for the state of New Jersey. Hoffman participated with the Houston Boxing Association with Josephine Abercrombie and promoted boxing events in Texas. He managed to get two champions to fight under their banner. One fighter was Frank Tate from Houston, the other was Joe Louis Manley from Illinois. I considered Hoffman and his wife good friends, and we often attended boxing matches together. He was familiar with the boxing scene and he helped the IBF during the development of our organization.

Arum knew Hoffman and I were close, so he would go through him to get to me for information regarding boxing matches, the fighters, or the ranking of fighters. There was a time that I would do anything for Hoffman because of his dedication to the IBF and all the positive things he had done for boxing. That's why I was upset to learn of the scam that he ran on me with the Foreman-Schulz fight. Hoffman had never asked me to do anything illegal. That's why I was so disappointed by his betrayal.

Ron Withers didn't have much contact with the IBF, but during his testimony, he claimed to have given a former commissioner in Nevada by the name of Elbert Durden around 10,000 dollars that was to be delivered to me from George Foreman. It allegedly was to be used to help with the expenses of the IBF's convention. Durden claimed that he never received money from Withers. Withers then changed his story and claimed to have given the money to my son on an encounter in Vegas.

They called Dino Duva to the stand, the son of Lou Duva who was a well-known trainer and manager of boxers for years. Dino Duva, his father, and late brother Dan had a boxing organization called Main Events Monitor, but after Dan died, Dino began to run the company along with Dan's former wife, Cathy Duva. They found out that Dino was allegedly skimming money off the top. They decided they were going to sever ties with him. Dino, Lou, and his sister Donna formed a new boxing organization called Lou Duva Boxing, leaving Main Event Monitor for Cathy to run.

Dino testified that around Christmas of 1999 there was a boxing match in Atlantic City at the Playboy Club, and I was invited to the match. My brother drove me to the fight. Afterward, we spent the night at the Playboy Club. In the morning we went down for breakfast and Lou Duva joined us along with a Dennis Dueltgen, a friend of Lou's. Dueltgen served as Lou's errand boy. While we were having breakfast Dueltgen received a phone call and excused himself to go meet with Dino. As we finished our breakfast and prepared to leave, Dueltgen approached me and said Dino told him to give me a present. I told Dueltgen to thank Dino and tell him Merry Christmas when he talked to him again. I took the bag home, placed it under the tree, and forgot all about it.

According to Dino's testimony, there was 25,000 dollars in the bag to thank me for the fights that I had approved. There may have been candy in the Christmas bag, I really don't remember, but I think I would have remembered a 25,000 dollars gift. Krovatin asked Dino if I had ever asked him for money and he said I hadn't. Krovatin asked Dino if he just gave me a bag of money just because he liked me. Krovatin didn't give Dino a chance to answer. He said he had no further questions.

When Dueltgen took the stand the prosecutor asked him about the bag that he had given to me. He said he did what he was told and gave the Christmas present to Bob Lee. The prosecutor asked him what was in the bag. Dueltgen said there was candy in the bag. The prosecutor asked him how he knew there was candy in the bag. Dueltgen admitted to being nosy and looking into the bag. During cross-examination, Krovatin asked Dueltgen why he thought Dino lied about the contents of the bag. Dueltgen said there was a rumor that Dino was on drugs and if he claims there was money in the bag, the rumors might be true.

By the time Dueltgen finished testifying, Dino Duva could do nothing but walk out with his head between his legs. It was the same old story, blame the Black man. There were a few other people who testified, including Roland Jankelson from Washington State. He had been a manager and promoter of Pinklon Thomas. His testimony was he had come to one of our conventions and wanted me to do whatever I could to get him and Pinklon on the same page. I told him there wasn't much that I could do about it. It was up to the ratings chairman. I had him meet with Beavers. He said he never received money from Beavers or me. He didn't help or hurt my case.

There was a fighter from Virginia who testified that he had been fighting under Duva's banner. He talked about wanting a shot at the title and explained how he thought the Duva's were good people. Krovatin cross-examined the fighter...

Krovatin: Do you know Robert Lee?

The Fighter: No sir, I do not.

Krovatin: Have you ever heard of Robert Lee?

The Fighter: Yes sir, I've heard of Mr. Lee, but I've never met him.

Krovatin: May I ask you why you are testifying?

The Fighter: Because they asked me to sir.

I believed it was for cosmetic effects because he was an African American and I believe they wanted someone who looked like me to testify against me. It would have made a little more sense if the man knew me. My attorney asked that his testimony be stricken from the record because his testimony had no value to the case. The fighter left the witness stand and went back to Virginia where he came from.

The IBF's treasurer, Bob Weitzel, one of the prime contributors to the formation of our federation was asked to testify, but because of his age and his health, he was excused. They brought in his wife instead. We paid Mrs. Weitzel to keep our books and monitor our financial business. The couple operated out of a small office in Portland, Oregon. All that she could testify to was how I made quarterly trips to Portland to go over the books with the accountant, her, and her husband. She couldn't tell much of anything else other than we paid her for services rendered. She also told them that I never touched the money unless a supervisor set the money in the office before it was sent to Portland. She had little impact on the case.

The FBI office in Portland, Oregon discovered during their inquiry into my case that the Weitzels had been skimming money off the top from the IBF. They were never charged with a crime and as far as I know never had to make restitution. The Weitzel's testimony before the grand jury was sealed, my attorney was unable to access the information. Through this entire ordeal, that was the hardest pill to swallow and to make it worse I was forbidden to talk to them per a court order. Take it from me, when you have people who are handling your money, you must check on them at least every three months. When people see the money, they can't help themselves, they must take some. The Weitzels presented me with flawless reports, but the reports had been doctored by Hugh McDonald a lawyer and accountant. Any time we would run low on cash, I would tell the Weitzels to keep my check to make sure our taxes were paid on time.

Bob and I had many things in common including both of us being Masons. I attempted to contact him years later to see how he was doing, but I couldn't reach him on the phone. I also attempted to reach Hugh McDonald to no avail.

CHAPTER 95

A correctional officer, I can't recall his name, was the next person on the stand. He worked in an upstate New York criminal facility. He moonlighted as a cornerman. Stan Hoffman got him the position. Hoffman testified that when Arum gave him money to give to me, he didn't want to cash the check in the US, he cashed it in the Netherlands. Then he said he brought the cash back into the country and supposedly gave me a cut. Of course, that never happened. Hoffman claims he gave the correctional officer a portion of the money to bring back to the US to hold until they got through customs. If you are traveling back to the US, you can't bring more than 10,000 dollars or you must report it to customs. Stan didn't want to get caught with that much cash in his possession.

The correction officer admitted that he knew what he was doing for Hoffman was against the law, but he did it anyway. He said that he gave Hoffman the money upon their return to the states and he knew to keep his mouth shut about the transaction. I don't know what happened to the officer, but I don't think anybody blew the whistle on him. If he worked for the government and he was laundering money, he should have been subjected to a substantial fine and perhaps some jail time.

The Caucasians: Arum, Withers, Hoffman, Duva, and the correctional officer according to their testimonies and the evidence against them violated the law, and most of them were able to continue with their participation in the sport of boxing. A friend said there must be a special place in Hell for all of them with Beavers being the chairman of the board. Although Brennan had been indicted, he was able to avoid the trial because of his failing health. They also indicted Francisco Fernandez, but because he fled to Columbia, they couldn't do anything to him unless he was foolish enough to return to the United States. The only two they chose to prosecute were the ones with a dark hue to their skin. My son and me.

Following the completion of the government's case, Krovatin proceeded to call character witnesses on my behalf. They vouched for me on my integrity as a businessman. They also vouched that I helped many minorities enter the boxing arena. It's sad to say that once I left the IBF, the recruitment of African Americans as officials has nearly ceased. That really ticked me off. After Krovatin finished with his examination of the witnesses, he rested his case.

When Krovatin gave his summation, he said the prosecution had failed to prove their case. He picked apart the testimony of everyone from the FBI agents all the way down to Withers and the correction officer. Despite everything the witnesses for the prosecution said they hadn't proved that I received any substantial amount of money from anyone. The only money that I received was the thousand dollars that Beavers returned to me from the loan.

The prosecution never turned over the so-called tape recording from a phone call between Beavers and me, but I have a feeling the tape didn't exist. Krovatin went on to say that his client never received anything from Don King or any other promoters.

When Krovatin finished his summation, he turned the floor over to Jose Sierra. He began to talk about how the government had proven their case and why the grand jury's indictment should be upheld. He said the trial had shown that I, Robert W. Lee Sr., was illegally involved in making sure that fights proceeded worldwide. Sierra discussed the envelope that I received from Beavers in the hotel room in Virginia. He said he believed Beavers was telling the truth about the money being a bribe, not a loan. Sierra briefly ran through the other testimonies of the prosecution's witnesses. Sierra made it clear that he was out to get Don King because he violated certain rules and procedures. He claimed to have found me complicit in the ratings scandals involving King. He believed that I should be convicted of the RICO Act violations for the crimes I allegedly committed.

Judge Bissell then gave his charge to the jury which lasted nearly an hour. It was obvious that Bissell seemed to be troubled by the presentation of the government, but he knew the case had to go forward. Krovatin said he believed that the verdict would either be a hung jury or an acquittal. He said if it wasn't, we were prepared to go to the Third Circuit Court of Appeals in Philadelphia to dispute the illegal search by the FBI. It frustrated me because it became a Black vs White trial. The only person of color that testified against me was the fighter from Virginia, and he didn't even know me. Most of the Caucasians involved in the trial for the prosecution either lied or perjured themselves and they walked away without any consequences.

CHAPTER 96

Not only did I receive a conviction, but my son and I also accrued massive attorney bills. We also had the expense of the bail money, ten thousand dollars apiece. There was a defense fund set up in my name to help with attorney fees. I don't remember exactly how much money was collected, but it was around five thousand dollars. Every penny of that money plus my savings went to defend my son and me. I fought for my freedom and lost. It was a glaring example to me how the scales of justice are imbalanced. She wears the blindfold saying justice should be blind and even. However, the truth is, in America no money equals no justice.

Arum testified without the benefit of an attorney saying he would accept whatever punishment they gave him. Of course, he never received any real punishment. I was told Arum was a former state's attorney and he still had a lot of connections in the US attorney's office in Washington DC. That's one of the reasons the prosecutor, Jose Sierra was soft on Arum during the trial. I knew he too was a part of the "Good Ol' Boys Club". The only consequence Arum received was having his promoting license suspended for six months by the Las Vegas Boxing Commission.

The headlines read Robert W. Lee, president of the International Boxing Federation, convicted of multiple violations of the RICO Act. They said the government had gone after the IBF, and they were going to indict me, arrest me, and destroy the IBF as we knew it. I felt Judge Bissell was fair with his summation and how he informed the jury on how to interpret the law. I don't think he gave me a break on any of the briefs that my attorney filed objecting to the illegally obtained evidence, because he sided with the government. I prayed that the jury would be able to see through some of the bias being shown toward the prosecution.

I was convicted on five counts. four counts for interstate travel and aid of racketeering surrounding the incident in Virginia. There was also one count of income tax evasion, even though I paid both my personal and the IBF's taxes promptly each year. We learned the jury dismissed 28 counts against me. Robert Jr. was acquitted of the five charges against him. He was free to go. Judge Bissell called my name and informed me that I would be sentenced later. He said that my attorney would inform me of when I needed to return to learn my fate. Bissell said he wanted me to understand that he was guided by federal sentencing laws. He said the length of my sentence will be mandated by the courts, not by him.

I received the call to be sentenced about two weeks before the Supreme Court handed down their decision. Judge Bissell sentenced me to the minimum, he couldn't go any lower. I believe he knew the government hadn't proven their case. With the jury of my peers containing nine Caucasians, that probably didn't help my case. I was sentenced to twenty-two months and Judge Bissell said they were revoking my bail, and sending me to Lewisburg Penitentiary in Lewisburg, Pennsylvania. I exhausted all my options, so I prepared to go to prison.

I had to report around noon on a Thursday to Lewisburg, my son drove me. We said our goodbyes and I entered the facility preparing for a world that was unknown to me. I went through processing, fingerprinting, and photographing. As I walked from one room to another some of the inmates called out to me saying they heard I was coming. I was encouraged by some of them to keep my chin up, they said that I would be okay. I waved to some and shook hands with a few as they led me to my room.

I talked to numerous inmates and they shared their personal horror stories about our so-called justice system. A few of them told me when they received their sentences of two to three years, the presiding judge would tell them they needed more time and would increase their jail time by a couple of years. I would ask them what their lawyers did to help them. I was shocked to learn that over 90% of them had public defenders who encouraged them to plead guilty to the charges. Unfortunately, the men had no other recourse and would have to serve the additional time.

ROUND 16

ONE MORE ROUND

CHAPTER 97

I wasn't in a penitentiary. I was in a camp where inmates were placed before they are released if they were good. There was more freedom, no fences, and a lot of wide-open spaces. There were about five guys who were sixty years or older. Most of the men were young, African American, or Hispanic. It was a warehouse of minority men. They had mostly been charged with possession of an illegal drug. Each of them had been encouraged by their public defender to cop a plea. The guys who were able to work were farmed out to some company. The guards would load them up on a bus around eight in the morning and they would return after a nine-hour shift. They were only making about two to three dollars per day repairing cell phones and televisions for the government to sell.

When I entered the facility, I was blind in one eye, and I had a problem with my foot because of diabetes. I was assigned the lower bunk because they knew I would have a hard time climbing onto the top one. They put me on medical disability because I was unable to do the jobs the other inmates were doing. I sat in my cell all day reading whatever I could get my hands on. I tried to mask my feelings while locked up, but I was feeling horrible about my situation and I couldn't believe this had become my life.

I still remember the first night sitting on the cot wondering what I was doing there. I felt an emptiness that I had never felt before. It reminded me of my time in the army during basic training, so I had been down a similar road. It was the knowledge that I was there for something that I didn't do that made me want to cry out. Although I knew no one would hear me.

When I arrived at Lewisburg an Italian guy asked me if I was Mr. Lee. I told him I was. He said that he needed to speak to me in private, so we took a walk. He said that he was getting out in a few days but wanted to tell me to be careful about who I talked to. He said there will be men who will ask about the federation, how you got started, about different fighters and information on Don King. He warned me that the camp was filled with men who would use any information they acquired to gain favor with prison officials. He said he heard I was a stand-up guy, the kind who wouldn't rat out his friends. He didn't want me to change that reputation by being a means to an end for some of the prisoners. I told him that I appreciated him looking out for my best interest. I only saw him one more time and that's when he was leaving prison for good. He pointed at me as he exited and told me to remember what he said. I wished him luck on the outside.

CHAPTER 98

I couldn't participate in any sports because of my leg and my vision. My days of playing baseball were over. I would still go out and watch the games, go to the weight room, and lift minimal weights. I didn't want to damage anything from my quadruple bypass. I read day after day and all through the night unless they would turn out the lights on me. I also participated in bible study and other church activities. I enjoyed discovering new authors such as Vince Flynn, who wrote a series of books about a fictional character named Mitch Rapp. Rapp was an agent known as a fighter for justice, like James Bond. I spent many hours in the prison library to help pass the time.

The payphone hung on the wall next to my bunk and I could hear the conversations of everyone who used it. I heard all the inmates' business. We were all one big family, but everyone had their own set of problems. I would hear about a family that had been evicted from their home, or desperate inmates trying to think of just one more person to help their family. Meanwhile, he's staring at seven more months in prison. I sympathized with the young men because I understood first-hand the flaws of our legal system and the pain it caused to our young men of color. I heard it all, from the inmate whining because he hadn't talked to his old lady in a long time, to the ones crying because they wanted to talk to their parents. The way they did Us was unbelievable, and this was the "good" part of the penitentiary.

There was a national movement to release prisoners who had been given inflated sentences. Prisons were becoming overcrowded due to a law passed by Reagan to lock up nonviolent drug offenders. They were loading them up by the busloads during the Reagan years. Young men were getting busted with a couple of joints just to make a cop's record more distinguished.

Krovatin went before the Third Circuit Court of Appeals and proceeded with an appeal to try to get my conviction overturned. There were two Italian judges and one African American judge all from the Pennsylvania area. Their names were McGee, Sciarra, and Alito. The two Italian judges ruled against me even though they knew it was an illegal search, and McGee, the African American judge, ruled in my favor. Sciarra and Alito determined that the trial judge was correct with his ruling. They let the film of Beavers removing the money from his sock into evidence, which helped to solidify the government's case. The conviction stood. They didn't want to retry me because their star witness, Doug Beavers, had died after the first trial. Without him, I would have walked out of that courtroom a free man. As strange as it seems, one of the judges from the Third Circuit Court named Sam Alito filled the vacancy on the United States Supreme Court a few years later. It was well known that they take care of their own.

After the Third Circuit Court wouldn't hear my appeal, my attorney appealed to the United States Supreme Court. There was a similar case on record against a woman named Sherry Singleton. There had been an illegal search that landed her in jail. They had a strong case against her that was overturned because the proper procedures weren't followed when searching her property. Krovatin felt if they overturned her case, they might do the same for mine.

A short time later when I was at Lewisburg, a fellow inmate told me that he read in USA Today that the Supreme Court refused to hear my case. I knew that I would have to serve the entire twenty-two months. A couple of government officials came to me saying that all of this would go away if I would give up the dirt on promoter Don King. This destroyed any trust that I had in the United States government. My refusal to lie on another African American man just to get out of my current situation is not who I am as a man. I felt as though the government took a shot at me, but they missed. It doesn't mean they weren't trying to kill me, it meant their aim was bad. Their actual target should have been the ratings chairman Doug Beavers.

After doing nineteen months of a twenty-two-month sentence, I was released early for good behavior. My time on the inside was uneventful, I stayed below the radar. I knew the government tried to break my spirit, but in the end, they gave me a sense of renewal, and I was able to face another day.

I was released from Lewisburg Penitentiary in February of 2006. Typically, when an inmate is released, they are placed in a halfway house, and they began to look for work. If they find a job, they are expected to pay a portion of their salary for "rent" to the halfway house and keep the rest for themselves. When I knew my release date was approaching, I petitioned my correction office to refrain from sending me to a halfway house due to my health and inability to seek employment. My vision had gotten worse, I had a heart condition, and my diabetes hadn't gotten any better. Plus, I had retired before going to Lewisburg. I remained at the penitentiary until my entire sentence had been served.

CHAPTER 99

M y son and my wife picked me up on my release date and took me home. It was a great day because I had been out of touch for nearly two years. It was great to ride in a car, to stop at a fast-food restaurant and to have lunch with my family. You don't realize the little things that you miss when you are locked away, I knew it was going to take a little while for me to be reacclimated to society and to return to life as I knew it. I quickly adjusted to the house that we purchased in March of 2004 only a couple of months before my July 24th incarceration date. Things remained pretty much the same aside from a few minor changes that my wife made around our home. It was great to be outside of the government's constraints.

I had to report to a federal probation officer out of Philadelphia. He and one of his assistants visited my home, interviewed my wife, and made sure that everything was in order. I also had to complete a monthly report and send it in, which I didn't find to be a problem. I was relieved to know that in a year I would no longer be on probation. Those 365 days couldn't pass soon enough.

I received a court order stating that neither my son nor I would be allowed to attend any professional boxing events; nationwide or worldwide. We were essentially blackballed from the sport that we knew and loved. I hadn't attended a boxing match since 1999 and would never be able to legally attend one ever again. This did not stop people who knew about me and the accomplishments that I made in the industry from calling and asking for advice. My phone rang with numerous people asking me questions like, which promoter they should use for their fighters, which managers were available, what training regimen to follow, and who were the best trainers. I gave them the best advice that I could, but I was always cautious because I never knew who might be listening in on the conversation. I didn't want to get jammed up for appearing that I was still involved in boxing.

I maintained a relationship with the people that I had previously worked with. Following my release, people from around the world contacted me to invite me to reside in their countries and create a new boxing organization. Although I thought about their offers, I knew that I didn't want to leave the United States. I knew that no matter how nice things would have been in other countries, there was no better place to be involved in boxing than the USA. The United States was the only place that I could become the first African American to form a successful international sports body that offered opportunities to everyone.

Many African Americans participate in many levels in various sports in the US, but none of them went on to become the head of an organization to direct traffic from the top. We were close to pulling the WBA and WBC into an umbrella situation where the three of us would be the organizers and the overseers of boxing worldwide. The people in other countries respected my authority and position of power. Many people in the United States were never in favor of it. They never wanted to see an African American with so much power. The other federations have issues both past and present that pale in comparison to what I was accused of, but due to the complexion of their skin, they were not held accountable for their deeds.

CHAPTER 100

Through it all, I felt like I left the IBF in good hands, but I did have problems getting them to honor benefits owed to me as the former president. The IBF was still in existence which showed a strong foundation. The commitment we had for helping people contributed to having a solid organization. While I was both proud and happy about the accomplishments that I made in the sport, I realized that it was time to move on.

I am a great believer in destiny and my path was being developed immediately upon my graduation from high school. The good Lord put his hand on me and began grooming me to be able to deal with people. My lessons began while I was working in a factory and having to communicate with all types of people daily. Then there was the police department which was very good training for improving my patience for dealing with the public. Each step was like climbing a ladder, going up a little bit higher until I reached the next level, which was the prosecutor's office. Becoming a lieutenant of investigators in Hudson County helped me to be a leader in difficult situations. The position at consumer affairs broadened my scope even further because I was able to identify the needs of my community and offer assistance to those who required help with everyday needs. Each step in my life I found it to be a learning experience.

In 2013 my wife threw me an 80th birthday party at a local restaurant, it was by invitation only. We received RSVPs from over 250 family members and friends. We had to limit the number of people attending because the restaurant owner said he couldn't accommodate more than 250 guests. People attended the celebration that I had known for years, some since my high school days. Many of the guests brought gifts and well wishes, congratulating me for reaching a milestone birthday. We only allowed a couple of people to speak during the tribute portion of the party because we didn't want to be there all night. Reverend Porter from my church said a prayer for those suffering from medical afflictions, for the blessings received by us all, and he blessed the food. We allowed a couple of other guys to speak, but we asked them not to get too political with their speeches. Several people worked with me when I ran for sheriff who came to extend well wishes to my family and me. Some of them jokingly asked me if I would like to come back to the force. I respectfully declined their offer, even though I knew it was said in jest.

CHAPTER 101

As I enter the Final Round of my life, I have to deal with my vision loss and the limitations placed on me by diabetes. I can no longer do some of the things that I love which includes landscaping my yard. I began going to lunch with some of the guys from the state commissioner's office every other month. They pick me up and we talk, laugh and joke at a neighborhood restaurant for hours.

My son comes from Fanwood twice a year to take me to a baseball game because he knows how much I love the sport. He takes me to see the Yankees, our favorite team. I can make out figures on the field, but my son tells me who they are. I love the atmosphere of the stadium. Eating hot dogs and the roar of the crowd take me back to the days when I attended baseball games with my brother when we were kids.

I don't have access to the media that provides details of boxing, but some people keep me informed on what's going on with the sport. Some are disappointed that I am no longer involved, I tell them it's time for the younger generation to make their mark on the sport. I'm grateful for every opportunity extended to me and I am excited to see the success that others are having in boxing. In some ways, I feel that in some way I contributed to their success. Sometimes I receive calls of people expressing gratitude for helping them reach their goals.

Not long ago a friend picked me up and took me to City Hall in Philadelphia where Lynn Carter, a judge that I appointed in the early 1980s, and taught her the ropes in the ring. She was inducted into the Philadelphia Boxing Hall of Fame. I was allowed to speak on her behalf. I received a standing ovation from the crowd along with a lot of handshakes and well wishes. That was the first boxing event that I had attended in nearly two decades. I went even though the court order was still looming over my head.

As the leader of the IBF and the USBA-I, I received many awards and accolades. One award that I received was given to me from a hospital in conjunction with an outdoor concert. I wanted to look my best, so I purchased a tuxedo. During the event, they honored me for my work with the International Boxing Federation. Smoking Joe Frazier and Michael Spinks attended the event. The cleaning crew, kitchen workers, and maintenance workers all joined in the celebration and tried to make their way over to meet Frazier and Spinks. Doctors and nurses from the hospital also joined in the festivities. I believed in the commitment of the hospital and its staff. I donated the money back that was a part of my award back to the cardiac unit at the hospital. After the concert, they had a spread fit for a king in the lobby of the hospital.

As of this writing, I am the only IBF charter member who is still alive. The others have gone to that big boxing ring in the sky. There were several things that we were proud of as an organization that was a benefit to boxing. The IBF was responsible for some very important changes to boxing. First, we mandated the use of thumb attached gloves in our championship bouts to prevent detached retinas. Then, we changed the weigh-in rules, changing them from the day of the fight to the night before the fight. We wanted the fighters to allow their bodies to rest and to be at full strength upon entering the ring for the fight the next day. The IBF also opened the door for some of the young aspiring boxers coming from the Union of South Africa who pleaded with us to recognize them. We did after the fall of apartheid. We were responsible for the formation of a forced savings account (boxers' pension) which helped boxers who fell on hard times. This account mandated that anyone fighting for one of our titles would have to give the IBF 2% of their prize money to be invested in a personal portfolio. Fighters were unable to access the money until they had been retired for at least five years.

I never ran into Don King again, although I did talk to him on the phone. Our paths don't cross anymore because he isn't as active in boxing and I'm not involved at all. I ran into Al Sharpton at an event where he was the speaker and we talked briefly. He laughed about his failed attempt to disrupt our convention many years earlier. I told him I remembered the maître d' was going to call the police on him. We had a good laugh about the incident. Sharpton and Martin Luther King III attended my trial to support me. Felix Trinidad from Puerto Rico, Evander Holyfield, as well as USBA champion Harold Knight showed their loyalty by attending the trial. The media asked them why they were there. They told them that I had done great things for boxing and had always done right by them.

People often ask me if Don King was aware of the witch hunt that was directed at him and if he knew what the government asked me to do. You can't be a Black man in America as vocal as King was and not realize there is a bounty on your head. I know that King knew that they were after him, but I told him that I wasn't a liar or a snitch. I wasn't going to put him in jail to save my rear, I knew how many fighters Don King had given a chance at a title and without him, many of the fighters would never have made it on the map. A report stated that King created twenty-three millionaires because he promoted them.

Robert Jr. went to work for a major cable company working out of Bloomfield and Marmouth County as an advertising accountant executive. He has done very well for himself. Robert was one of twenty people that were recognized as being the best sellers of advertising. He was number one in his zone and attended a conference in Mexico that celebrated his accomplishments. People were lining up to work with him because of his success in the company. He attributed some of his success to working with Arum, Duva, and especially King. Robert Jr. said he took a page from their book and used it to get ahead in the corporate world.

As I reflect on my life while writing my memoirs, I remember the prophecy of Miss Mable when she said: "I's not saying he ain't gon' have trouble, but he will always come out smelling like a rose." The fact that I am still alive and have my freedom lets me know that she was right.

I hope that young people will be inspired to use whatever abilities they have to consistently look forward; never backward. I want them to realize that there may be obstacles that are placed in their path, but you have to go around, through, or over them. Don't stop! I encourage the younger generation to know that as the old spiritual says, "There's a bright side somewhere don't you stop till you have found it. There's a bright somewhere."

A WORD TO ASPIRING BOXERS

If you are an aspiring boxer seeking a world championship title, here is some knowledge from someone who knows the sport like the back of my hand. First, get in the gym and make sure that your body is fit and ready for the rigors of hand-to-hand combat. Secondly, when people around the gym notice your talent and offer you a contract, be on your toes. If someone wants to be your manager and presents you with a contract sit with your family and an attorney to ensure that you are completely familiar with the language and duration of the contract. Finally, I urge you not to sign with a manager for more than three years at a time. If the marriage between the manager and the fighter is good, you can renew for another three years. If it is a bad relationship you have the opportunity to seek alternative representation. These tips will help you be your own advocate and less likely to be taken advantage of while pursuing your dreams in the sport of boxing.

I dedicate these memoirs to the following International Boxing Federation charter members who started with me on this journey.

Jersey Joe Walcott	International Commissioner
James Stevenson	Vice President
James Rondeau	First Vice President
Hiawatha Knight	Second Vice President
Mike Cusimano	Third Vice President
Alvin Goodman	Fourth Vice President and Co-Legal Council
Walter Stone	Legal Council
Jack Battalia	Medical Director
Bill Brennan	Championship Chairman

Arch Hindman	Executive Secretary
Frances Walker	Ratings Chairman
Robert Weitzel	Treasurer

Awards:
New Jersey Boxing Hall of Fame Inductee
Washington DC Boxing Hall of Fame Inductee
Atlantic City Boxing Hall of Fame Inductee
NAACP -Benjamin Hooks Award
Lou Costello Award
Newark -New Jersey City Council Award (Two-time award)
British Boxing Board of Control Award
Hungarian Boxing Commission Award
Russian Boxing Commission Award
Italian Boxing Commission Award
Spanish Boxing Commission Award
Philippine Boxing Commission Award
South Korea Boxing Commission Award
Member of the Board of Managers for John Runnells Hospital
Member of the Board of the Union County Psychiatric Clinic
Member o the Board of the Union County Mental Health Committee
Member of the Urban League
Member of Scotch Plains- Fanwood Human Rights Council
Member of the New Jersey Diabetes Council
Good Friday Presbyterian Concert Award

Randy and Kathleen Neuman and Robert W. Lee with his daughter Cheryl Lee

IBF Convention in Atlanta, Georgia (1995)

Roy Johnson {New Jersey Chief Inspector} and Bob Lee

Bob Lee with Comedian and Actor Redd Foxx

Nicaraguan Boxer Alexis Arguello

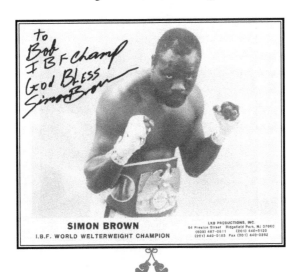

To
Bob
I B F champ
God Bless
Simon Brown

SIMON BROWN
I.B.F. WORLD WELTERWEIGHT CHAMPION

LKB PRODUCTIONS, INC.
94 Preston Street   Ridgefield Park, NJ 07660
(609) 467-0511   (201) 440-5120
(201) 440-0183 Fax (901) 440-0282

New Jersey Governor William T Cahill {1970-1974} and Robert W. Lee

Robert W. Lee first African American Police Officer in Scotch Plains, New Jersey

Boxer Evander Holyfield and Robert W. Lee

CHERYL ANN LEE

Cheryl Ann Lee August 4 1965-October 21, 1998

Jersey Joe Walcott, Robert W. Lee, and Reginald Fox {1992}

Robert W. Lee ran for the position of Sheriff in Union County {1971}

Robert W. Lee at his USBA -IBF office

Robert W. Lee leading a USBA Executive Committee Meeting Washington
DC {1979}

New Jersey Boxing Commissioner Inspector Lindsey Tucker, Bobby Lee,
Frank "The Animal" Fletcher, and Bill Wisner {1991}

Robert W. Lee, Fred "The Hammer" Williamson, and Eddie Bunn {1990}

Robert W. Lee